Advance Praise

"Generative AI tools have changed every industry that involves creativity, a blank screen, and an idea to get started, online courses included. Thankfully, Danny Iny is one of the brightest minds in how to build a better course, and how to use Generative AI tools to take them to another level. If you create any kind of course, this book is not only timely but critical to your success. Start here; you will be thankful that you did."

—MITCH JOEL, CO-FOUNDER OF THINKERSONE AND AUTHOR OF *SIX PIXELS OF SEPARATION* AND *CTRL ALT DELETE*

"There is no doubt that AI is already dramatically impacting the online course business. The real question is how and—more importantly—what to do about it. As usual, Danny Iny is leading the way with answers. This book is a must-read for course creators who want to stay ahead of the curve and learn to leverage what may be one of the most important technologies of our lifetimes."

—JEFF COBB, AUTHOR *LEADING THE LEARNING REVOLUTION* AND FOUNDER OF LEARNINGREVOLUTION.NET

"Skillfully demystifying AI, this book offers tangible ways to elevate online courses to new heights. If you're a coach, consultant, or expertise-based entrepreneur, read it now so you can better navigate the future."

—DORIE CLARK, AUTHOR OF *THE LONG GAME* AND EXECUTIVE EDUCATION FACULTY, COLUMBIA BUSINESS SCHOOL

"Danny's abilities as a futurist, strategist, and online course entrepreneur are first-class. Learn from Danny and his team to accelerate your results exponentially."

—CHRIS BADGETT, CEO OF LIFTERLMS

"Brilliantly bridging the gap between online courses and AI, this book is an essential read for coaches and consultants who want to thrive in our fast-changing environment. Discover the future of efficient, impactful, and AI-enabled course creation."

—RON KAUFMAN, AUTHOR OF *UPLIFTING SERVICE*

"This book is a welcome corrective to the (mostly empty) hype about AI for online marketing and online courses. Sure, AI can be powerful—but like any powerful tool, it's easy to use it incorrectly and shoot yourself in the foot (digitally speaking). That's why you need this essential new book. Danny and his team explore how coaches, speakers, and independent course creators can leverage the power of AI to reach new clients, develop richer content, and accelerate their marketing. Take a break from playing around with ChatGPT and read this book!"

—ABE CRYSTAL, CEO OF RUZUKU AND AUTHOR OF
THE BUSINESS OF COURSES

"Technology is redrawing the field of play for thought leaders, and this book is the road map that each of us need to ensure that we take advantage of what AI has to offer while also letting our expertise shine through."

—LAURA GASSNER OTTING, AUTHOR OF *WONDERHELL*

"*I consider Danny to be the #1 authority when it comes to where the online course industry is headed. When Danny talks, you'd be wise to listen . . . or watch the effect on your bottom line if you don't.*"

—JONATHAN LEVI, FOUNDER OF SUPERHUMAN ACADEMY
AND AUTHOR OF *THE ONLY SKILL THAT MATTERS*

"*No topic evokes fear and fascination as profoundly as artificial intelligence. Millions want to know what it is, whether it can help me, and if it is a fad, or worse, if I am a course creator, will AI wipe me out? Enter Danny Iny and his team. They deliver a synthesized, knowledgeable, and exceptionally pragmatic guide to how artificial intelligence can work for us. Rarely is a book useful for almost everyone, but this one can help any person engaged in creating courses, or anything else.*"

—CONSTANCE DIERICKX, AUTHOR OF *META-LEADERSHIP*

"*If you're a coach or consultant looking to stay top of mind with clients, this book brilliantly demonstrates how AI can transform your business. If you've got valuable expertise to share, this book will help you learn how AI can help.*"

—DAVID BURKUS, AUTHOR OF *BEST TEAM EVER*

"*ChatGPT and its many cousins might just be the tool that takes your training from good to amazing. This book can be a compass and a map to help navigate the brave new world that awaits.*"

—MICHAEL BUNGAY STANIER, AUTHOR OF *THE COACHING HABIT* AND *HOW TO WORK WITH (ALMOST) ANYONE*

GUIDE
on the SIDE

WINNING WITH COURSES IN THE AGE OF AI

Danny Iny | Ari Iny
Heather E. Wilson | Elizabeth Lee

MIRASEE PRESS
P.O. Box 24540
West Hill
Montreal, QC
H4B 3A5, Canada
www.mirasee.com

Hardback ISBN: 978-1-7373742-9-9
Paperback ISBN: 979-8-9891641-0-3
E-Book ISBN: 979-8-9891641-1-0
LCCN: 2023917294

Printed in the United States of America
1 3 5 7 9 10 8 6 4 2

For Dave Lakhani, who left us all too soon. Rest in peace, my friend.

—Danny

This book is dedicated to my family: my wonderful and supportive wife, May, and our adorable baby, Hannah.

—Ari

To all the course creators out there striving to create more freedom and make a positive impact in the world: your legacy will transform generations to come. And to Larry, my beloved soulmate, thank you for always believing in me.

—Heather

To all the people, too many to list, who have helped shape me into who I am, especially my wife and children, who fill my life with joy and silliness.

—Elizabeth

Contents

From Expert to Visionary, Embracing the AI Revolution

IN 2003, I embarked on an exciting journey, building and selling my first online course. Ever since, I've been challenging conventional wisdom and introducing new ways of thinking and being that reshape people's understanding of the world around them. Throughout the past two decades, I've leveraged these innovative strategies to author books as well as build and sell businesses.

During this time, technology has revolutionized networking, business models, hiring processes, marketing and sales strategies, and more. The internet, smartphones, and social media have driven change at a whiplash pace. Now, artificial intelligence (AI) is reshaping the business landscape, raising a flurry of questions:

- Where can I integrate AI while maintaining the integrity of my work?
- In what areas can AI outperform me?
- How can I leverage AI without compromising the quality of my work?
- Should I be concerned about being replaced by AI?

I'm not worried about AI replacing you or me. AI can answer any question Google can. However, it can't ask questions, seek hidden truths, or develop new ideas. Not yet, at least.

Currently, AI is like an ultra-efficient intern, programmed to execute tasks swiftly but lacking the discernment to evaluate the accuracy of its results or explore more effective methods. It's a powerful tool, but like any intern, it requires guidance and supervision.

AI is impressive when it comes to handling routine tasks and ensuring things run smoothly. In fact, it has already started taking over some job responsibilities, leading to concerns that AI might soon replace experts in various fields.

But wait, didn't I just say that I'm not worried about AI replacing us? That's right. You see, I'm not an expert—I'm a visionary. And if you consider yourself an expert, it might be a good idea to think about making a shift. It might be time for you to venture out of Expertville and start spending more time in Visionary Town. At least visit and see if it's for you.

Let me explain why.

Before AI became the next big thing, platforms like YouTube provided a way for experts to share their knowledge with anyone with an internet connection and a smartphone. It enabled experts to reach a wider audience, and it also gave ordinary folks the chance to become experts themselves. Initially, this increased the demand for expertise.

However, over the last decade or so, there has been a massive influx of experts. The supply of experts has grown much faster than the demand, resulting in a decrease in their value. It's reasonable to think that AI might contribute to further devaluing expertise in the coming years.

While it's uncertain how exactly AI will shape the future, one thing remains true: When you help others see the world through a new lens, you've already made a significant leap into the realm of visionaries. So, rather than worrying about the potential impact of AI, focus on harnessing your visionary abilities to make a difference in this evolving landscape.

What's the difference between an expert and a visionary?

An expert shares today's best practices, which often define the status quo. But as best practices evolve, experts find themselves in a perpetual pursuit of the ever-changing status quo.

A visionary, on the other hand, challenges the status quo and offers a new or alternative approach that changes the way people see the world. While an expert reflects today's reality, a visionary paints a picture of what the world could look like tomorrow and far into the future.

This is why visionaries like Malcolm Gladwell or Brené Brown can create a course or write a book that tops the charts for decades, while a subject matter expert needs to produce a new course or book every year as the previous year's best practices become outdated.

Danny Iny is a visionary. As a leading voice in the world of online courses and education, he's been challenging the status quo and offering new ways of seeing work, solving problems, and approaching business growth. This book is a testament to that.

Can you be a visionary?

Yes. But it may require approaching your work with a blank piece of paper and a beginner's mind. To find new ways of solving problems, you may need to let go of old methods and beliefs. But you can start your journey to Visionary Town today by asking a few questions:

- What's the biggest problem in my industry?
- What's the status quo approach to solving this problem?
- Is there a better way to solve this problem?
- Do we need to think differently about the problem?
- Is the problem the real problem, or is it actually a different problem?

Questions like these, and many others, will lead you on a journey of exploration and investigation into the seemingly intractable problems faced by the people you serve. As a visionary, your job is to find new and more effective solutions to those problems. Not just "how to" solutions but "how to think" solutions.

Experts offer solutions to problems already solved; visionaries ask questions Google can't answer.

The Visionary Quest Matrix

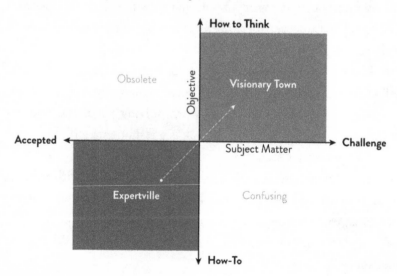

©The Visionary Quest Matrix. Reproduced from *The Referable Speaker* by Michael Port & Andrew Davis

If the overpopulation of experts has already devalued expertise, AI could potentially amplify this trend even further. While I can't predict the future, I can confidently assert that when you embark on a journey of guiding others to see the world differently, you have already taken a significant leap out of Expertville and into Visionary Town.

As this book will reveal, AI can be a fantastic tool for accelerating your business development. AI excels at:

- Data Analysis
- Pattern Recognition
- Natural Language Processing (NLP)
- Image and Speech Recognition
- Automation of Repetitive Tasks
- Predictive Analytics

AI can help you produce faster and more efficiently, for sure. But, did you notice what *isn't* on this list?

- Challenging the status quo and offering new or alternative approaches
- Helping people see the world differently
- Giving people the hope and inspiration they need to make better choices and lead more meaningful lives
- Changing the way people feel

AI can serve as your efficient assistant, but it's up to you to guide its course, challenge traditional thinking, and envision a unique path forward. Some may sit back skeptically, waiting to see how the

AI evolution unfolds. You have the opportunity to be a pioneer and experiment with innovative tech tools and envision the realm of possibilities. AI can be a valuable tool to support your visionary work.

How am I so certain you can do this?

Because you're human. You possess the unique traits of empathy, curiosity, and creativity. Above all, you care. Your concern for others sets you apart.

If you want to change what people do, you need to change how they think. If you want to change how they think, first you need to change how they feel. AI can give people the information they need and it can tell them what to do, but it can't change how they *feel* about that information. That's your job.

Let your passion and compassion be the driving forces on your visionary quest in search of new solutions to difficult problems.

Think big,

Michael Port
Co-Founder, Heroic Public Speaking
New York Times and *Wall Street Journal*
best-selling author of nine books, including
Book Yourself Solid, Steal the Show, and *The Referable Speaker*

Finding the Script

IN A JUST AND FUNCTIONING SOCIETY, we each have a role to play; politicians serve the interests of their constituents, bankers keep our money safe, and the police are there to serve and protect. But it doesn't always work out that way. Some police officers become the very villains they were supposed to protect us from, recent decades have seen predatory lending scandal after scandal, and too many politicians care only about growing their power and lining their pockets.

When we drift from the role that we're supposed to play, we've "lost the script." When athletes become so obsessed with winning that they resort to cheating and doping, they've lost the script. When institutions of higher learning reimagine themselves as luxury brands that brag about how many people they turn away, they've lost the script. And when entrepreneurs devolve into caricatures of Ebenezer Scrooge or Monty Burns, they've lost the script too.

I'm not an expert on politics, banking, or police reform, but I do know a thing or two about business—especially the business of online courses. For over a decade, my company, Mirasee, has helped coaches, consultants, and other expertise-based entrepreneurs shift from the traditional trading of dollars for hours to the leveraged transformation of online courses. We show them how to help a lot more people in a much more leveraged way, which grows both their impact and their income.

That's the fundamental script for online course entrepreneurs: to help more people get ever better results from your knowledge and expertise. And yes, of course, you make money in the process—often lots of it! But my experience has shown me over and over that business is about more than just making money; it's about creating a sustainable way of making the impact you care about seeing in the world. And profitability is an important part of it—otherwise it wouldn't be sustainable—but it is a means to an end, rather than the end itself.

This might sound a bit idealistic, but it's true. Ask any successful entrepreneur who has poured their heart and soul into a business. They will tell you that if all you want to do is make money, there are much easier, more consistent, and more reliable ways to do it! Being an entrepreneur means being driven by the instinct that something can be better—you see a problem, inefficiency, or misalignment, and you have a nagging sense that with a bit of luck and elbow grease, you can make it better.

And yet the entrepreneurial imagination is too easily captured by shiny marketing tools promising disproportionate returns. That's how artificial intelligence tools (like ChatGPT) first came onto my radar—as one of those tools that promises to change the game by "automagically" doing large swaths of the work for you, faster and better than you could yourself!

I was skeptical; after all, experience has taught all of us that if it sounds too good to be true, it probably is. But I started looking deeper . . . and deeper . . . and even deeper. And I quickly came to three important realizations. First, there is a "there" there—this is real, and course creators (and everyone, really) will ignore it to their extreme professional peril. Second, AI is much more than just a time-saving vehicle. This technology really is going to change everything about the way we all work. But the real kicker was the third realization: that this is fundamentally different from just about any marketing or productivity technology we've seen before. This is true on many levels, which we'll explore throughout this book.

With most marketing and business innovations, the impact of their misuse or abuse is very limited, usually just disappointing results. It's like the old fable of the tortoise and the hare; the overeager-to-get-rich-quick-via-shortcuts-and-loopholes jackrabbit tends to run out of steam well shy of the finish line, whereas the slower-but-steady-and-focused-on-value tortoise builds the lasting education empire. No big disappointment for anyone other than the jackrabbit.

The story with AI is more complicated. Misuse that stems from ineptitude can be business-endangering for the entrepreneur doing it, which is reason enough to get this right. But the bigger impact that we all need to be aware of is the inevitable abuse of AI technologies at the hands of entrepreneurs who will lose the script of what they're supposed to be doing—drawn by the siren song of "passive income" and "making money while you sleep." That inevitable abuse is going to have cataclysmic impacts on the online courses industry, fundamentally changing the realities in which we all operate. It's as if the overeager jackrabbit were trying to save time by catching a ride on a nuclear missile—no tortoise will escape the fallout!

This is no exaggeration. If anything—and as you'll see in the coming pages—I'm understating the risk and impact. That's why it is vitally important that we all understand and leverage AI through the lens of the script of what it really means to be an online course entrepreneur: teaching your gifts so that you can empower more people to fix whatever problem your expertise is well poised to fix, and making the world a little bit better in the process. And of course, doing it all profitably!

Ari Iny, Heather E. Wilson, and Elizabeth Lee know the importance of keeping to this script, which is why I asked them to co-author this book with me. We each bring a unique and complementary perspective from our work and experience helping course entrepreneurs to grow their business. Mine is the 30,000-foot perspective on the online course business journey and our industry as a whole from my perch as founder and CEO of Mirasee. Ari, in addition to being my brother, is the Head of Strategy for our ACES Business Acceleration program, which has given him a bird's-eye view of over a hundred online expertise-based businesses. Heather, as our Director of Education who leads our team of course-building coaches, has been intimately involved in the daily blocking and tackling of helping online course entrepreneurs to realize their visions. And Elizabeth, as our resident instructional designer and course developer, has the most (and most recent) experience actually building courses for today's marketplace. In a world where so many seem to have lost the script, none are better equipped than Ari, Heather, and Elizabeth (and myself) to help you find it.

What you hold in your hands (or listen to through your earbuds) is the product of our collaboration: our best attempt at a definitive account of what AI really means for the online courses industry. We'll show you exactly where these technologies fit (and don't fit) into the various parts of your business, and also how the landscape is changing in response to these technologies—as well as what you need to do to adapt, and stay ahead. So without further ado, let's begin. And thank you for entrusting us to guide you on this journey.

Danny Iny
Founder/CEO at Mirasee
Author of *Leveraged Learning*,
Online Courses, and *Teach Your Gift*
July 2023 | Montreal, Canada

Note to the Reader

BEFORE DIVING into the heart of the matter, here's a quick note about you, technology, us, and the structure of this book.

About You—While we'll speak at length about AI, we're assuming that you aren't here simply to geek out about how emerging technologies are the coolest thing since sliced bread. Rather, our expectation is that your focus and interest is on how you can teach your gift through the vehicle of online courses, to create leverage, freedom, and impact in your business and life. So while we will go deep into the topic of AI, it will always be through that lens.

About Technology—While this book is about the impact of AI on the world of online courses, and we will go into a fair amount of depth about some important current technologies, this isn't a technology book per se. Rather, this is a book about the world of online courses and how it is being disrupted by AI (and what you need to do in order to navigate the challenges and seize the opportunities that are emerging).

About Us—This book is co-authored by four people, who all work together at the online business education company Mirasee: Danny Iny (founder and CEO), Ari Iny (Head of Strategy for the ACES Business Acceleration Program), Heather E. Wilson (Director of Education), and Elizabeth Lee (Lead Course Developer). Generally, we'll refer to ourselves collectively as "we" or "us," but in passages about a specific co-author, we'll refer to them by name (e.g., "online courses changed Danny's life" or "when Heather was a young girl").

About the Structure of This Book—We've divided this book into three broad parts:

- **Part 1: AI and Online Courses**—We begin by getting to know the relevant technologies, and how they should (and shouldn't) be used to create online courses and build online businesses.

- **Part 2: The Modern Course Opportunity**—Here we explore the landscape of online courses, which has been fundamentally changed by the advent of AI technologies.

- **Part 3: Your First Hybrid Course**—This is your road-map to building and launching your first (or next) profitable online course, with the assistance of AI.

All right, enough with the disclaimers—turn the page, and let's dive in!

Claim Your Free "Online Courses and AI" Success Bundle

We've created a special bonus resources package to support you in applying the ideas in this book to build and launch your own online course business:

✓ **Hybrid Courses Bootcamp video training series**

✓ **Audiobook of Danny's bestseller *Effortless***

✓ **Library of our most commonly used AI prompts for course building**

This entire resource bundle is our no-cost-whatsoever gift to you.

→GO TO MRSE.CO/GUIDE-RESOURCES TO CLAIM IT!

PART 1:
AI and Online Courses

CHAPTER 1

The Overnight AI Revolution

"Companies in every industry need to assume that a software revolution is coming."

—*Marc Andreessen*

IN ERNEST HEMINGWAY'S NOVEL *The Sun Also Rises*, the character Mike Campbell is asked, "How did you go bankrupt?" His response? "Two ways. Gradually and then suddenly."

This line captures the larger truth that change tends to happen in small increments that are barely noticeable, until they add up to a huge shift that appears to come out of the blue. Whether it's something catastrophic, like a bankruptcy; a popular fad; or a person's "overnight success," change drips away in the background, often for many years, until, in the blink of an eye, something is very different.

How did you get divorced? Gradually, then suddenly. How did you fall asleep? Gradually, then suddenly. And how did artificial intelligence revolutionize the online courses industry? Gradually, then suddenly.

A BRIEF HISTORY OF AI

Artificial intelligence isn't a new idea—in fact, it's been around since antiquity! One of the earliest examples of an artificial being is the golem, which, in Jewish folklore, was a creature made of clay brought to life through mystic rituals and able to carry out tasks given to it by its creator. In ancient Greek mythology, the god Hephaestus created automata, or self-operating machines, that helped him in his work as a blacksmith. He also created Talos, a giant bronze man, to protect Crete from invaders. And in Hindu mythology, the god Brahma created manasputras, the first humanlike beings, out of his thoughts.

And in the last century, legends and stories gave way to more concrete work. During World War II, researchers working on code-breaking and other military projects developed some of the earliest electronic computers. These machines were primarily used for numerical calculations, but their creators also speculated about the possibility of creating machines that could think and reason like humans.

One of the earliest thinkers to explore this concept of intelligent machines was Alan Turing, the English mathematician. In a 1936 paper, Turing proposed the concept of a "universal machine" that could be programmed to perform any computation that could be carried out by a human. During World War II, Turing played a key role in breaking the German Enigma code.

In the 1940s and 1950s, researchers continued to explore the possibility of creating machines that could reason like humans. This led to the development of the more sophisticated electronic computers, which were used to perform complex calculations and data analysis. During this time, researchers also began to experiment with neural networks, which are computer systems designed to simulate the way the human brain works. They hoped that this approach would enable machines to learn from experience, rather than being programmed with explicit rules.

In the 1960s and 1970s, researchers made significant strides in the development of natural language processing and machine learning. Natural language processing involves teaching computers to understand and interpret human language, while machine learning helps computers learn and improve over time. These are both foundational aspects of modern AI systems.

Things didn't always develop smoothly. The 1980s brought an AI winter, as the promises of AI researchers failed to materialize, leading to disappointment and a loss of confidence in the field. This was due in part to the limitations of the technology of the time, which made it difficult to build truly intelligent systems. Funding for AI research dried up, and many researchers left the field.

Then, in the 1990s, a new wave of AI research began, fueled by advances in computer hardware and software. One of the key breakthroughs in this era was the fuller development of machine learning, which has been used to create some of the most impressive AI applications in recent years, including image recognition and autonomous vehicles.

Thanks to decades of advances, today AI is being used in a wide range of fields, from health care and finance to entertainment and education. Speech recognition technology has enabled voice assistants like Siri and Alexa to understand and respond to human commands. Language translation tools powered by AI have made it easier to communicate across different languages and cultures. AI-powered robots are increasingly used in manufacturing, while AI-based medical diagnosis tools are helping doctors to make more accurate and timely diagnoses.

And yet, as ubiquitous as AI has become in recent years, it didn't really break into the popular consciousness until the very end of 2022.

GRADUALLY: HERE COMES OPENAI

While the latest chapter of AI really kicked into gear in late 2022, it began quite a bit earlier: on December 11, 2015, when a group of prominent figures in tech including Elon Musk, Peter Thiel, Reid Hoffman, Sam Altman, and others pooled a billion of their dollars to found an organization called OpenAI. They set to work building a technology that they dubbed the Generative Pre-trained Transformer—which became abbreviated to just GPT.

So what is it, exactly, that they had built? Well, translating from computerspeak to English, a generative pre-trained transformer is essentially a statistical prediction engine built on top of a large language model (LLM). We realize this still sounds like computerspeak! But the truth is that you're probably familiar with some simpler language models.

Auto-complete is one such language model. Many mobile devices today have built-in keyboard apps that include a predictive text feature. These features use language models to predict the next word that you are likely to type based on the words you have already typed. These predictions can be based on a variety of factors, including the context of the sentence, your typing history, and your personal writing style. For example, if you frequently type "coffee" on your phone, the language model may learn to prioritize that word in its predictions when you start typing "c-o-f." But if you're a funeral home director, odds are that you've typed "coffin" more than "coffee," so the model will prioritize "coffin" for you.

If you have your phone nearby, go into your text messages and type "I am going to the . . ." What does your phone suggest next? "Store," "gym," "gas station," "doctor," "office"? Everyone is going to get slightly different suggestions. That's because your phone is using an AI language model to predict the most likely next word in your sentence based on what it knows from what you have typed previously.

Now try another one: "The aardvark sat on the . . ." Unless you're a zoologist, this is a phrase that you likely haven't typed before! What does your phone suggest? Instead of using your previous history, your phone's language model is going to use what it's learned generally about human language. Where do people or animals usually sit? On the floor, the ground, the couch, and so on.

Most of the prediction engines we're used to are children's toys compared to GPT—whereas your phone keyboard app predicts a few options for the next word, and Google might propose a dozen different ways to complete your search query, GPT auto-completes the entire answer to whatever question you pose to it.

As if that weren't impressive enough, OpenAI then built a chatbot technology on top of the GPT statistical prediction engine. They called it ChatGPT, and it allowed for a few very powerful capabilities. We'll explore them in more detail later in the book, but by far the most important innovation was that it allowed users to query the GPT engine using natural language—so instead of typing a bunch of computer code, you could just ask it a question in plain English.

To say that the technology was impressive would be a massive understatement. And yet, it flew mostly under the radar. Then came November 30, 2022, a landmark day in the history of artificial intelligence. On that day OpenAI introduced version 3.5 of its GPT engine, and made ChatGPT available to the public . . . and all hell broke loose.

THEN SUDDENLY:
THE WORLD MEETS CHATGPT

Everyone, from high school students looking to avoid writing an essay to programmers looking to debug their codes, heard about ChatGPT and wanted to use it. And use it they did! The platform attracted over a million users in just its first week, and reached the one hundred million user mark in just two months—faster adoption than any other technology in history. For context, the next fastest technology to 100 million users was TikTok, which took nine months, and Facebook, which took over four years.

Time to reach 100 million monthly active users

No. of Months

Platform	No. of Months
Chat GPT	2
TikTok	9
Instagram	30 (2 years, 6 months)
Pinterest	41 (3 years, 5 months)
Spotify	55 (4 years, 7 months)
Telegram	61 (5 years, 1 months)
Uber	70 (5 years, 10 months)

ChatGPT's ability to generate humanlike responses, with a memory able to handle everything from basic inquiries to in-depth back-and-forth conversations, got people very excited. Its applications seemed endless. Companies and individuals from many different fields hopped right on the bandwagon. AI had been around for decades, but now, suddenly, everything felt different. ChatGPT had the potential to revolutionize entire industries!

Content creators started using ChatGPT to generate content for various industries, including blogs, social media platforms, and e-commerce sites. News agencies like the Guardian and Reuters have even used ChatGPT to create automated news articles.

ChatGPT was being used to develop medical chatbots and virtual assistants to help patients with various health issues. For example, a start-up called Cass developed a chatbot that uses ChatGPT to provide mental health counseling to users, and another start-up called Osmosis developed an AI-based tool to help medical students learn and review key concepts.

Game developers were using the platform to create more immersive and engaging gaming experiences, such as generating new quests. And because ChatGPT's output sounds so human, these developers could also create non-playable characters (NPCs) that respond to players in real time, based on whatever is happening in the game. And that only scratches the surface.

Danny first started hearing about ChatGPT in December of 2022, and his first reaction was to dismiss it. Something to know about Danny is that he doesn't usually jump on hot new technologies. As of this writing, he has never been on TikTok or Instagram (though at one point his team did create an account for him). He watched Clubhouse come and then go, without ever bothering to see what the fuss was about. And his instinct was to do the same with ChatGPT, but the more he heard and the more he saw, the more he realized that this wasn't one of those things he could just watch go by. So he started playing with the technology, and understood viscerally just how impactful it was going to be—which, of course, is why you're reading this book right now.

This is no fad. Generative AI had "gradually" laid the foundations for change, and now it was "suddenly" disrupting every industry it touched—from entertainment and gaming to health care and finance, and everything in between. And it wasn't just ChatGPT, either. Out of nowhere, the internet was suddenly awash with AI tools promising to solve any problem you could think of.

THE NOT-SO-WIDE WORLD OF AI

If you want to start a business that will grab attention and inspire investors to write you a check, there's a simple formula to follow: take an old problem that is felt by large numbers of people and solve it in a (presumably better) way using a shiny new technology. Many of the companies that you transact with every day grew out of exactly this sort of simple formulation, such as Amazon (buying stuff + e-commerce), Uber (hailing a ride + smartphones), and Airbnb (finding a place to stay + peer-to-peer marketplace).

Occasionally the new invention is completely homegrown; Google built its search business, for example, on the back of their co-founders' innovative PageRank algorithm. But usually companies piggyback on somebody else's technology innovation (Amazon didn't invent e-commerce, Uber didn't invent smartphones, and Airbnb didn't invent peer-to-peer marketplaces), which is why every major technological innovation (the internet, mobile smartphones, blockchain) brings with it a Cambrian explosion of new businesses using it to solve all sorts of problems.

Given the disruptive capabilities of generative AI, it's no

surprise that the market has become flooded with start-ups using it to solve any number of problems. Want help drafting a letter? There's AI for that. Do you have a video to edit? There's AI for that. Need a photo to go with your blog post? There's AI for that too. And the list goes on, and on, and on, and on some more. It's a very, very long list!

And it can all be very confusing. Should you use ChatGPT? Or Notion AI? Or Jasper? Or Copy.ai? Or Grammarly? Or Sudowrite? Or Microsoft Copilot? Or Bing? Or Bard? Or Claude? Or Pi? Or one of the hundreds (if not thousands) of other tools out there?

Even if we wanted to, there's no way that we could compare and contrast all the tools out there *today*, never mind keep recommendations up-to-date as the landscape evolves. But we can guide you in sorting the wheat from the chaff yourself—and it helps a lot if you understand a little bit about the technological architecture of all these tools. That's what we'll share with you in the rest of this chapter, with one disclaimer: None of us are AI engineers, and we're assuming that if you're reading this, you aren't either. So what follows is a dramatically oversimplified layperson's explanation, but it should give you insight that will help you make sense of how this world is structured.

Understanding LLMs: Mary had a little . . . what?

We've already begun to explore how generative AI is essentially a really elaborate version of auto-complete—predicting the statistically most likely response, one next word at a time. And there's some fancy algorithmic wizardry that goes into running those probabilities, but all the algorithmic wizardry in the world can't overcome the critical limitation that plagues both artificial and non-artificial (a.k.a. human) intelligence, which is that in order to learn, we need something to learn *from*.

Consider the phrase "Mary had a little . . ."—most of us probably know that the 'correct' next word would be "lamb," but that's just one of an almost infinite array of words that would work both conceptually and grammatically (for example, "problem," "headache," "sandwich," or "free time"). We know that the next word is probably "lamb" because we've heard the nursery rhyme. But what if we'd never heard it? We could speak perfect English and have an IQ of 160, and still just not know that what Mary probably had was a lamb!

Generative AI tools get the information that informs their statistical predictions of all those next right words from the LLM that they're built on top of. And the word *large* is a bit of an understatement—in fact, these models are mind-bogglingly ginormous. GPT 3.5, which is the version that basically broke the internet when it was released in 2022, was trained in 17 gigabytes of data and spanned 175 billion parameters. GPT 4, which was released a mere 104 days later, expanded the pool to 40 gigabytes of training data and 100 *trillion* parameters. And among all that data and complexity is the knowledge that Mary did in fact have a little lamb:

Complete the sentence "Mary had a little . . ."

lamb, its fleece was white as snow.

To clarify, OpenAI didn't make the model so big just for bragging rights; it's the size of the model that makes the results so good. So for the AI to be any good, the language model has to be very large—and the larger the model, the more expensive to assemble, and to query, which is why there aren't very many of them. And they are all built and owned by pretty much exactly who you would expect:

either huge companies with very deep pockets (Google, Meta, etc.) or extremely well-funded start-ups (OpenAI, Anthropic, etc.).

But this raises a question: If there are so few LLMs out there, how can there be so many AI tools coming on the scene every day?

The Interface: A Thin Layer of Innovation

The GPT prediction engine that OpenAI built is very impressive, but it isn't just the power of the underlying technology that pushed it into the mainstream. In addition to the GPT prediction engine that sits on top of a giant LLM, there is also ChatGPT, which is an interface layer that sits between the user (you) and the underlying generative AI technology. So you don't need to type in obscure computer commands or learn to write code. Instead, you can just ask ChatGPT your question in plain English (or whatever language you like), and ChatGPT will send your query to the prediction engine that is informed by the trillions of parameters in the LLM.

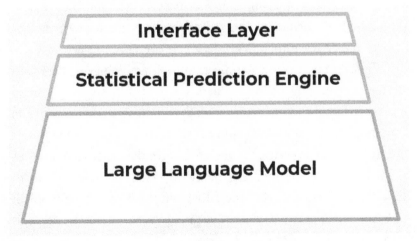

Some LLMs are proprietary, meaning that the only way to access them is through the tools that the company that built and owns it has chosen to offer. But some LLMs (notably the OpenAI GPT engine) also offer application programming interfaces (APIs) that allow other developers to build their own interface layer to access them. And that's what the vast majority of AI tools out there are doing; they act as a middleman between you and ChatGPT, querying the same prediction engine that sits on top of the same LLM.

This intermediary feature could be as simple as just putting your prompt through verbatim, but usually there's a bit more to it than that. Imagine, for example, that you had a friend who was uncomfortable with technology to the point of not feeling comfortable posing a simple question to Google or Alexa. They might ask you the question instead. And if you don't know the answer, you could turn around and repeat the exact same question to the technology that could serve up the answer. But you would probably change the question a bit to a format that would be more likely to garner a helpful response. For example, if your friend asked you if eggs are a good source of calcium, you might reformulate that for Google into a search query along the lines of "calcium content of eggs."

That's pretty much what most AI tools are doing—taking your prompt and passing it on to ChatGPT, with some added context as a preceding paragraph to (hopefully) improve the quality of the response. For example, you could ask ChatGPT to "write me a sales letter for my yoga service," or you could give the exact same prompt to an AI copywriting tool. Both tools will pass that query down to the GPT prediction engine and LLM, but the copywriting tool will probably add a bunch of context, such as copywriting frameworks to follow and examples to model.

"Write me a sales letter for my yoga service"

AI Copywriting Tool
"Here are copywriting frameworks to follow..."
"Here are examples of sales pages to model"

ChatGPT

Now, in fairness, this explanation isn't intended to take away from the value that some of the tools offer. As we'll explore in later chapters, the quality of the prompt has enormous impact on the quality of the results, which makes better prompts often worth paying for. And the previous explanation is a bit reductionist—sometimes tools will also do things like ask questions and then use the answers to write additional questions in a loop, leading to (hopefully) better answers for you.

Lipstick on a Beautiful Pig

We've done a whirlwind tour of the technological architecture underlying the plethora of AI tools. They're all different interface layers, and they're all querying the same (very small number of) statistical prediction engines and LLMs. For some readers, this chapter will have been fascinating, and for others it may have felt tortuously technical. So why did we include it in the book?

The reason is that AI is going to be such an important part of all of our businesses and lives, so it is important to have a basic vocabulary to help us all understand what really is (and isn't!) on the table, and how much of your energy really needs to go into investigating every new tool that crosses your path.

As the saying goes, you can put lipstick on a pig, but it's still a pig. Well, AI is a beautiful pig, and the lipstick of different interface layers can help to bring out some of that beauty—but fundamentally it's the underlying technology that really matters. Will some tools be better than others? Of course! But it will be differences of degree, and what matters more than anything is learning where and how to use them to support your business. And for that, we need to understand what AI really can (and can't) do for us.

CHAPTER 2

When Online Courses Met ChatGPT

"Oh, it's alive! It's alive! It's alive!"
—*Victor Frankenstein*

BY THE TIME you hold this book in your hands (or listen through your earbuds), odds are that you will have long since created your own ChatGPT account and experimented with all the different things that you can ask it to do—in which case, you probably already have a good sense of how and why this technology will impact our industry.

But just in case you haven't and you're still thinking, "But what's the big deal about all this technology and what can you even do with it?" this chapter is your answer. It's a verbatim transcript of an early "test drive" exchange that Danny had with ChatGPT when he was trying to feel out what it could do.

Now, keep in mind that while Danny is an accomplished course creator (and fast typist!), he'd be hard-pressed to produce much more than one thousand words of course material per hour. The following transcript (more than three thousand words) took a paltry 10 minutes and 34 seconds to produce. And this was done at the very start of 2023. Since then, the technology has gotten smarter and faster. As you'll see, it took mere minutes to settle on a course topic, create an outline, and draft lesson scripts, sales pages, marketing emails, and more.

It isn't perfect by any means—and we'll explore the exact nature of those imperfections in later chapters. But even so, reading the transcript will give you a visceral sense of just how powerful the technology is.

CHATGPT CREATES A COURSE IN 10 MINUTES

I am a business and marketing coach. What are 10 topics for courses that someone like me could sell?

As a business and marketing coach, here are ten topics for courses that you could potentially sell:

1. Marketing Strategies for Small Businesses: This course could cover how to create effective marketing strategies for small businesses, including social media marketing, email marketing, and advertising.
2. Building a Successful Online Business: This course could cover how to build and grow an online business, including topics such as e-commerce, website design, and search engine optimization.
3. Sales and Negotiation Skills: This course could cover the fundamentals of sales and negotiation, including how to identify customer needs, handle objections, and close deals.
4. Personal Branding: This course could cover how to develop a strong personal brand that will help you stand out in your industry and attract more clients.

5. Content Marketing: This course could cover how to create and distribute valuable content that will attract and retain customers, including topics such as blogging, video marketing, and podcasting.

6. Business Planning and Strategy: This course could cover the basics of business planning and strategy, including how to develop a mission statement, set goals, and create a business plan.

7. Customer Service and Satisfaction: This course could cover how to provide excellent customer service and increase customer satisfaction, including topics such as handling complaints, resolving conflicts, and creating customer loyalty.

8. Social Media Marketing: This course could cover how to use social media to promote your business and engage with your audience, including topics such as social media advertising, influencer marketing, and community management.

9. Time Management and Productivity: This course could cover how to manage your time effectively and increase your productivity, including tips for prioritizing tasks, minimizing distractions, and staying focused.

10. Leadership and Team Management: This course could cover how to be an effective leader and manage a team, including topics such as communication, motivation, and conflict resolution.

Let's go with sales and negotiation skills. What are 15 different titles that I could use to call this course?

Sure, here are 15 different titles you could use to call a course on sales and negotiation skills:

1. Mastering Sales and Negotiation: Strategies for Success
2. Art of Persuasion: Mastering Sales and Negotiation Skills
3. The Ultimate Sales and Negotiation Masterclass
4. Effective Sales and Negotiation: Techniques and Best Practices
5. Closing the Deal: Sales and Negotiation Strategies for Professionals
6. The Science of Sales and Negotiation: Tools and Techniques for Success
7. Boost Your Sales and Negotiation Skills: A Practical Approach
8. Advanced Sales and Negotiation: Elevate Your Results
9. Power of Persuasion: Essential Sales and Negotiation Skills
10. The Negotiator's Advantage: Techniques for Success
11. The Sales Professional's Guide to Successful Negotiation
12. The Winning Formula for Sales and Negotiation
13. Achieving Sales Excellence through Effective Negotiation
14. The Art and Science of Sales and Negotiation
15. Closing with Confidence: Mastering Sales and Negotiation Skills

Let's go with Closing the Deal. Outline for me a 6-week curriculum for this course.

Sure! Here's a possible 6-week curriculum for a course titled "Closing the Deal" that focuses on mastering sales and negotiation skills:

Week 1: Introduction to Sales and Negotiation
- Understanding the sales process and the importance of negotiation skills
- Building rapport with customers and understanding their needs
- Effective communication skills for sales and negotiation

Week 2: Building Trust and Establishing Credibility
- Establishing trust and credibility with customers
- Understanding the power of active listening and empathy
- Developing effective questioning techniques to uncover customer needs

Week 3: Negotiation Strategies and Techniques
- The art of negotiation and persuasive language
- Developing effective negotiation strategies to achieve win-win outcomes
- Handling objections and managing difficult customers

Week 4: Sales Presentations and Demonstrations

- Creating and delivering effective sales presentations
- The importance of visual aids, storytelling, and testimonials
- Overcoming objections during sales presentations and demonstrations

Week 5: Closing the Deal

- Effective closing techniques to seal the deal
- Understanding customer buying signals and behavior
- Techniques to handle customer hesitations and close more sales

Week 6: Follow-up and Relationship Building

- Understanding the importance of follow-up after the sale
- Building and maintaining relationships with customers
- Managing customer feedback and referrals for continued growth

Of course, this curriculum is just one possible outline and can be adjusted to meet the needs of your specific audience and teaching style.

Great. Can you write me a script for the first week's lesson?

Sure! Here's a possible script for the first week's lesson, "Introduction to Sales and Negotiation":

Hello and welcome to the "Closing the Deal" course! In this first week, we'll be exploring the world of sales and negotiation, and why it's such a critical part of any successful business.

So, what is sales? At its core, sales is the process of identifying a customer's needs and providing a solution to meet those needs. But in order to do that successfully, you need to have strong communication skills, a solid understanding of your customer base, and the ability to build rapport and establish trust.

That's where negotiation comes in. Negotiation is the art of finding a mutually beneficial solution, and it's a critical part of the sales process. Whether you're negotiating a deal with a new client or working to keep a current one, you need to be able to navigate the negotiation process with confidence and skill.

So, let's start with the basics. The first step to successful sales and negotiation is building rapport with your customers. That means taking the time to understand their needs, and making a personal connection. You want to show your customers that you care about them, and that you're there to help them find the right solution for their needs.

One of the most important aspects of building rapport is effective communication. You need to be able to listen actively and communicate clearly to be able to identify your customers' needs and convey your proposed solutions. One key element of effective communication is using open-ended questions, which encourage your customers to share more information with you.

Another important element of sales and negotiation is establishing credibility. You want your customers to trust you and your expertise, so they're more likely to take your recommendations and buy from you. There are a few ways you can establish credibility, including showcasing your experience, providing relevant case studies, and obtaining endorsements from current or past customers.

In summary, sales and negotiation are critical skills for anyone in business. You need to be able to identify your customers' needs, communicate effectively, build rapport and establish credibility, and navigate the negotiation process with confidence. Over the next few weeks, we'll be diving deeper into these skills, and exploring the strategies and techniques that can help you become a master at closing the deal.

Great. What would be a short assignment that I can give people at the end of the lesson to complete?

For an assignment to accompany the first week's lesson, "Introduction to Sales and Negotiation," here's a short activity that could help students practice building rapport and asking effective questions:

1. Identify a friend or family member to interview.
2. Prepare a list of open-ended questions to ask during the interview. Try to avoid questions that can be answered with a simple "yes" or "no."
3. During the interview, practice active listening and ask follow-up questions to gather more information.
4. Reflect on the interview and identify any opportunities to build rapport or establish credibility, such as sharing a personal experience or providing a relevant example.

The purpose of this assignment is to help students practice the communication and listening skills that are essential for building rapport with customers. By interviewing someone they already know, they can focus on honing their skills without the pressure of a sales environment. This activity also allows students to reflect on their interview and identify areas for improvement, which can be helpful in future sales and negotiation situations.

Okay. We can come back to outlining the rest of the course later. But I also have to sell it. Can you write a short sales page for the course?

Sure! Here's a possible short sales page for the "Closing the Deal" course:

Are you struggling to close deals with potential customers? Do you feel like you're not reaching your full sales potential? If so, you're not alone. Closing deals is one of the most challenging aspects of business, and it requires a unique set of skills that not everyone possesses.

That's where the "Closing the Deal" course comes in. This 6-week course is designed to help you master the art of sales and negotiation, so you can achieve better results and grow your business. Through a combination of interactive lessons, activities, and group discussions, you'll learn how to build rapport with customers, ask effective questions, and navigate the negotiation process with confidence.

Whether you're a seasoned sales professional or just starting out, this course will provide you with the tools and techniques you need to close more deals and achieve greater success. By the end of the course, you'll be equipped with a comprehensive understanding of the sales process, and you'll have the confidence and skills to handle any sales or negotiation situation that comes your way.

Here's what you can expect to learn in each week of the course:

- Week 1: Introduction to Sales and Negotiation
- Week 2: Building Trust and Establishing Credibility
- Week 3: Negotiation Strategies and Techniques
- Week 4: Sales Presentations and Demonstrations
- Week 5: Closing the Deal
- Week 6: Follow-up and Relationship Building

This course is perfect for business owners, sales professionals, entrepreneurs, and anyone who wants to improve their sales and negotiation skills. Don't miss out on this opportunity to take your business to the next level—sign up for the "Closing the Deal" course today!

Great. I'd like to beef this up with 10 "fascination" bullets of specific things that they'll get from the course. These bullets should ideally spark some curiosity.

Sure! Here are 10 "fascination" bullets that you can use to beef up the sales page for the "Closing the Deal" course:

1. Discover the secret to building rapport with

customers, so you can create stronger connections and win more deals.

2. Learn how to establish credibility with your customers, so they trust your recommendations and become loyal customers.

3. Explore the power of effective communication, and uncover techniques that will help you identify your customers' needs and provide targeted solutions.

4. Master the art of negotiation, and learn how to find mutually beneficial solutions that leave both parties satisfied.

5. Learn the key elements of an effective sales presentation, including visual aids, storytelling, and testimonials, to close more deals.

6. Discover effective strategies for overcoming objections, handling difficult customers, and closing deals with confidence.

7. Gain a comprehensive understanding of the sales process, from building rapport to follow-up, so you can streamline your approach and achieve better results.

8. Identify your unique strengths as a salesperson, and learn how to leverage them to your advantage.

9. Find out how to identify buying signals and customer behavior, so you can be more effective in your sales and negotiation efforts.

10. Develop a powerful set of skills and techniques that will help you achieve better results and grow your business, no matter what industry you're in.

These fascination bullets are designed to pique the reader's curiosity and make them interested in learning more about the course. By highlighting specific benefits and outcomes that they can expect from the course, you can generate excitement and anticipation for what's to come.

Okay. I'll also need a good headline for the sales page. Can you propose 10 different options?

Sure! Here are 10 different headline options you could use for the sales page:

1. Close More Deals and Grow Your Business: The Ultimate Sales and Negotiation Course
2. Discover the Secrets to Sales and Negotiation Success with "Closing the Deal"
3. Elevate Your Sales Game: Master the Art of Closing Deals
4. Unleash Your Inner Sales Pro: Learn the Techniques of the Pros
5. Dominate Your Sales and Negotiation Game: Get the Skills You Need to Succeed
6. The Sales and Negotiation Course that Will Change Your Career
7. Close Deals with Confidence: Master the Art of Sales and Negotiation
8. Unlock Your Full Sales Potential: "Closing the Deal" Course Starts Now
9. Gain the Confidence and Skills to Close Any Deal with the "Closing the Deal" Course

CHAPTER 2: **When Online Courses Met ChatGPT**

10. Accelerate Your Sales Success: Discover the Techniques of Top Sales Professionals with "Closing the Deal"

Great. I also want to have a sales video at the top of the page. Can you write me a script for that sales video?

Sure, here's a possible script for a sales video to accompany the "Closing the Deal" course:

OPENING SHOT: A busy office environment, with people on the phone and typing on computers. An enthusiastic voiceover begins to speak.

VOICEOVER: "Are you tired of losing out on deals? Do you struggle to find the right words when negotiating with potential clients? If you answered yes, then you're not alone. Closing deals can be one of the most challenging aspects of business, but it doesn't have to be."

Cut to a shot of a person on the phone, looking flustered and frustrated.

VOICEOVER: "Imagine feeling confident in your ability to close deals and negotiate with ease. Imagine having a powerful set of skills and techniques that you can use to win over even the toughest clients. That's what the "Closing the Deal" course is all about."

Cut to a shot of a person leading a sales presentation, looking confident and engaging.

VOICEOVER: "This 6-week course is designed to help you master the art of sales and negotiation, so you can achieve better results and grow your business. With a comprehensive curriculum that covers everything from building rapport to closing the deal, you'll gain the confidence and skills to handle any sales or negotiation situation that comes your way."

Cut to a shot of a person sitting at a desk, taking notes and looking engaged.

VOICEOVER: "Our experienced instructors will guide you through interactive lessons, activities, and group discussions, giving you hands-on experience and personalized feedback to help you achieve your goals. And the best part? You'll be part of a community of like-minded professionals, so you can share your experiences and learn from others."

Cut to a shot of a person shaking hands with a satisfied client.

VOICEOVER: "So, if you're ready to take your sales and negotiation skills to the next level, don't miss out on this opportunity to join the "Closing the Deal" course. Sign up today and start your journey to success!"

CLOSING SHOT: The course logo and website URL appear on the screen. The voiceover repeats the website URL and invites viewers to sign up.

Great. I'd also like to have a series of 5 emails that I can send to potential prospects, telling them about the course and inviting them to sign up. Can you outline that sequence for me?

Sure! Here's a possible sequence of 5 emails you can send to potential prospects, designed to provide more information about the "Closing the Deal" course and generate interest in signing up:

Email 1: Introduction and Course Overview

- Briefly introduce yourself and your business.
- Give an overview of the "Closing the Deal" course, including its focus on mastering sales and negotiation skills.
- Highlight some of the key benefits and outcomes that students can expect from the course, such as increased confidence, more closed deals, and better relationships with customers.

Email 2: The Importance of Building Rapport

- Highlight the importance of building rapport with customers, and how it's a critical aspect of successful sales and negotiation.
- Provide some examples of how building rapport has helped you in your own business or career.
- Tease some of the specific strategies and techniques that students will learn in the course for building rapport and establishing trust.

Email 3: The Art of Persuasion and Negotiation

- Discuss the art of persuasion and negotiation, and how it's a key part of the sales process.
- Provide some examples of how effective negotiation has helped you close deals and achieve success.
- Tease some of the specific negotiation strategies and

techniques that students will learn in the course, such as finding mutually beneficial solutions and handling objections.

Email 4: The Power of Sales Presentations

- Discuss the importance of effective sales presentations, and how they can be a powerful tool for closing deals.
- Provide some examples of how effective sales presentations have helped you in your own business or career.
- Tease some of the specific sales presentation strategies and techniques that students will learn in the course, such as using visual aids, storytelling, and testimonials.

Email 5: Closing the Deal and Follow-Up

- Discuss the importance of closing the deal and follow-up, and how they're essential components of successful sales and negotiation.
- Provide some examples of how effective follow-up has helped you in your own business or career.
- Highlight some of the specific closing techniques and follow-up strategies that students will learn in the course, such as identifying buying signals and managing customer feedback.

In each email, be sure to include a clear call to action and a link to the course website where they can sign up. By providing valuable information and teasing specific strategies and techniques, you can generate interest and excitement in the course, and encourage more prospects to sign up.

Can you write out the first email for me?

Sure, here's an example of the first email in the sequence:

Subject: Introducing "Closing the Deal" -
The Ultimate Sales and Negotiation Course

Hello [Prospect's Name],

My name is [Your Name], and I'm a business and marketing coach who specializes in helping professionals like you improve their sales and negotiation skills. Today, I wanted to introduce you to my new course, "Closing the Deal."

The "Closing the Deal" course is a comprehensive 6-week program designed to help you master the art of sales and negotiation, so you can achieve better results and grow your business. Through a combination of interactive lessons, activities, and group discussions, you'll learn how to build rapport with customers, ask effective questions, and navigate the negotiation process with confidence.

Here are just a few of the key benefits you can expect from the course:

- Increased confidence in your sales and negotiation abilities

- A comprehensive understanding of the sales process, from building rapport to follow-up
- A powerful set of skills and techniques to help you close more deals and win over tough customers

Whether you're a seasoned sales professional or just starting out, the "Closing the Deal" course has something to offer. Our experienced instructors will guide you through every step of the process, providing personalized feedback and hands-on experience to help you achieve your goals.

If you're interested in taking your sales and negotiation skills to the next level, I encourage you to sign up for the "Closing the Deal" course today. You can find more information and sign up at [Course website URL].

I look forward to working with you and helping you achieve your sales and negotiation goals.

Best regards,

[Your Name]

CHAPTER 3

The Power (and Limitations) of AI

"The way I see it, if you want the rainbow, you gotta put up with the rain."

—*Dolly Parton*

A MAJOR CHALLENGE of our time is knowing what to believe and how strongly to believe it, particularly when it comes to new tools and technologies that some people have a vested interest in seeing succeed.

Consider three of the most overused words in the hypester's toolbox: "This changes everything." They're a go-to for every entrepreneur who wants you to adopt their belief in the value of their product or invention. And there's a self-fulfilling dimension to these proclamations, in that if everybody actually buys into the idea, the impact will be a lot greater than it otherwise would have been. Which is why marketers use those three words to describe all manner of products, and sometimes even paint themselves into a corner and have to go back to the well, as Apple did in marketing the iPhone 4: "This changes everything. Again." Sheesh.

Of course, the more people line up to tell us that everything is going to change, the more weight we might give the claim. So the fact that we are hearing about the disruptive effects of AI from swaths of entrepreneurs, technologists, commentators, and politicians from across the ideological spectrum should count for something.

But the funny thing is that the more something actually does "change everything," the less any of us need to be told. We just *know* it, from our own firsthand experience. And for most of us, the very first time you got to play with a generative AI tool, you had the same feeling that Danny did when he first took it out for a spin to test its course-building chops; his mind was racing with ideas about how much time AI would be able to save with tasks like finding the right course topic, coming up with outlines and content ideas, brainstorming exercises, drafting marketing materials, and finding where to reach target clients. And that was just the beginning.

It also raised some scarier questions, like what happens when all our competitors have this technology? What if they learn to use it before we do? And what happens if and when the market gets flooded with information that we thought only we could provide, but now it looks like it's all inside the AI? There's a truism in business that if the rate of change outside your business is faster than the rate of change inside your business, then pretty soon you're going to be out of business. And there's no question that the mainstream introduction of AI technologies was the starting gun to a much faster race across many industries, which might be why so many companies are rushing to implement AI into every part of their operations, without fully understanding any of the implications!

And while it might seem silly and rushed, there's a strange logic to it. The introduction of AI to knowledge industries is a bit like the introduction of electricity and power tools to the trade of carpentry. Imagine being the only carpenter who *doesn't* start using power tools—you'd be out of business, and fast! And the same is true if you're the only course builder who doesn't leverage AI—your courses will take dramatically longer to deploy, and they won't be nearly as

© marketoonist.com

good as the ones that your competitors will offer. And when it comes to the marketing—they're going to lap you there too!

So let's explore exactly how the world of course building will be changed by generative AI—which is different from what you might imagine, and different from what a lot of the AI hype suggests. And to understand where this incredible technology will take us, we have to start by understanding its limitations.

THE STOCHASTIC PARROT

Way back in 1950, mathematician and AI theorist Alan Turing proposed a threshold for evaluating whether an artificial intelligence is, in fact, intelligent. There's some nuance to it, but it more or less boils down to a human's ability to tell whether they're talking (well, typing) to another human versus to a computer. This came to be known as the Turing test.

Now, the most generous graders would argue that the Turing test was passed as far back as 1966, by Joseph Weizenbaum's ELIZA program. And even the most stringent evaluators will agree that modern LLM-based generative AIs are well past that point. But it turns out that this isn't just a measure of how good AIs have become—it's also a measure of how bad human beings are at assessing the intelligence (or lack thereof) that is built into the tools we interact with. In fact, we're so bad at it that we can't help but use anthropomorphizing language to describe it!

But the truth is that *artificial intelligence* is a bit of a misnomer, in that most AIs aren't actually intelligent—at least, not the way that humans are. But they are good at mimicking intelligence, thanks to two important factors: first, the LLMs that drive them, and second, the stochastic nature of their algorithms. Google Dictionary defines *stochastic* as "having a random probability distribution or pattern that may be analyzed statistically but not predicted precisely." In other words, even though these LLM-based AIs are all statistical prediction engines (like a fancy auto-complete), they won't return their answers in exactly the same way each time. For example:

Please write a 100 word bio of Abraham Lincoln.

Abraham Lincoln (1809–1865), the 16th President of the United States, served during one of the nation's most challenging periods, the Civil War. Born in a log cabin in Kentucky, Lincoln's humble beginnings did not deter him from becoming a self-educated lawyer and a respected politician. His Emancipation Proclamation in 1862 initiated the end of slavery, a landmark moment in U.S history. Lincoln's legacy as a symbol of unity and his principled leadership, exemplified in his Gettysburg Address, endure today. Tragically, he was assassinated by John Wilkes Booth just days after the war's end in 1865.

And again, just a few minutes later:

Please write a 100 word bio of Abraham Lincoln.

Abraham Lincoln, born February 12, 1809, is revered as one of America's greatest presidents. Born into poverty in a Kentucky log cabin, Lincoln rose to become the 16th President of the United States, serving from 1861-1865. His tenure was marked by the Civil War, a period during which he preserved the Union and abolished slavery via the Emancipation Proclamation. Lincoln is also celebrated for his eloquent rhetoric, notably the Gettysburg Address. His life was tragically cut short when he was assassinated by John Wilkes Booth in April 1865. Lincoln's legacy remains etched in American history as a leader of courage, compassion, and integrity.

See how the answers aren't quite the same? That's what stochastic means. And you can try it yourself—if you ask ChatGPT for a "100 word bio of Abraham Lincoln," it won't be identical to either of the above responses. The stochastic quality of these AI-generated responses goes a long way to creating the illusion that you're dealing with an intelligence that really understands your question and its answer, except neither of those things are true.

It doesn't "understand" what you are asking it, and it doesn't even "understand" what it tells you in response. It's just statistically predicting words, which is why LLM-based generative AIs are sometimes called "stochastic parrots." Now, to be clear, it often does a really good job—clear, coherent, accurate, and even funny and insightful—but that won't always be the case. Sometimes it will be very deeply, misguidedly wrong.

Garbage In, Garbage Out

We opened the first chapter in this book with a quote from Hemingway's *The Sun Also Rises*:

"How did you go bankrupt?" Bill asked.

"Two ways," Mike said. "Gradually and then suddenly."

Now, several of us have read Hemingway, and we got the quote straight from the source. But just for fun, we also asked ChatGPT, which told us that Mike was talking to Jake, not Bill. It also told us that Bill said, "I went bankrupt, slowly, and then all at once." Which might have been close enough for our purposes, but it wouldn't be right. This quote confusion happens for two important reasons, which help us understand the most important limitation of generative AI:

1. It is about prediction, rather than retrieval; it doesn't go out and look for the right answer to your question. Rather, it just predicts what the right answer should *sound like*— not what it actually is!

2. The prediction isn't based on carefully curated source information (which in this case should be Hemingway's original manuscript); it's based on its entire library of training data, which for ChatGPT is the entire internet.

For GPT 3.5 it's the internet up to September 2021, and newer versions are more current. But the training data isn't curated—it's all the internet. Since Hemingway's line is paraphrased and misquoted all over the internet, it's not surprising that ChatGPT didn't get it quite right.

There's a popular phrase in computer science: "garbage in, garbage out." It basically means that the quality of the output of a computer program is directly related to the quality of the input code or data. If you put garbage in, you can't expect roses to come out. And this isn't just about the stuff that is inflammatory or discriminatory, which many AIs do try to filter out. The bigger issue (for our purposes) is the grab bag of random people's ill-considered opinions and "facts" that are just plain wrong.

So what happens when you have an LLM that includes at least a portion of garbage data, and it informs an AI that stochastically predicts what the next right word should sound like (rather than what it is)? You get answers that sound great, but may not actually be correct. To illustrate what we mean, we'll share the result when Danny did the AI-equivalent of Googling himself, which is asking ChatGPT to write your bio. Here's what it wrote:

Write a bio of Danny Iny.

Danny Iny is an entrepreneur, author, and speaker who has established himself as a leading voice in the world of online education and marketing. He was born in Israel in 1980 and grew up in Montreal, Canada.

Iny started his career in technology as a software developer and consultant, working with clients such as Microsoft, Google, and IBM. He later turned his attention to online education and founded his company, Mirasee, in 2011. Mirasee provides training and coaching for entrepreneurs who want to build successful online businesses.

Iny has authored several books, including *Teach and Grow Rich* and *Engagement from Scratch!*, both of which focus on creating successful online courses and engaging with audiences. He has also been featured in numerous publications, including Forbes, Inc., Entrepreneur, and Business Insider.

In addition to running Mirasee, Iny is a popular speaker who has delivered keynote speeches at conferences around the world. He is known for his engaging and informative presentations on topics such as entrepreneurship, marketing, and online education.

Iny is also a dedicated philanthropist and serves on the board of several non-profit organizations. He currently lives in Montreal with his wife and three children.

It sounds good, doesn't it? And it says the sort of things that you would expect to be true of someone who is a CEO and author. And parts of it are true—but there are also a lot of inaccuracies; Danny was neither born in Israel nor in 1980. He didn't begin his career as a software engineer, and never did any work with Microsoft or IBM. He doesn't do much speaking, nor does he serve on any non-profit boards. Oh, and he has only two children.

So what does this mean for ChatGPT's reliability? Very simply, if you feed it internet junk, that same junk might come back out. The internet isn't *all* garbage, of course; it's a mixed bag. We think it's fair to say about ChatGPT: "mixed bag in, mixed bag out." This isn't to say that it can't be a very powerful tool for course creation and business growth. It absolutely can—but you have to use it the right way.

YOUR TIRELESS DIGITAL ASSISTANT

Analogies are useful. You could share a 142-minute account of a kind and simple man from Alabama to illustrate the capricious serendipity of life ... or you can just say that "life is like a box of chocolates, you never know what you're going to get." By the same token, while rules and checklists for using AI in your course building can be helpful (and we'll get there), we can shorten the learning curve substantially with a good analogy—one that helps us get our heads around the right and wrong way to use generative AI in our course and business building. And the best analogy that we've come up with is to think of generative AI as an infinitely hardworking, but only *reasonably* competent, assistant.

Imagine that you had such a person on your payroll, arriving bright-eyed and bushy-tailed to their first day of work. They are tireless, dedicated, super-efficient, and never offended when you tell them that the work is wrong and they have to redo it. But they don't have real expertise, or an ability to think for themselves. You can't trust their judgment. Such a person would still be a great asset to your business—just so long as you keep your hands on the wheel, and you're ready to take control when needed.

We've polled thousands of entrepreneurs, asking them how they would work with such an assistant. The answers are always the same, and mirror our own thinking: you would give them hyper-specific instructions, and you would always check their work.

Hyper-Specific Instructions, A.K.A. Prompt Engineering

If you were born in the sixties, you might remember a time when room-sized computers were programmed using punch cards. Or if you're a child of the seventies or eighties (like the authors of this book), you probably remember being told about those punch cards in the "in my day" stories of your older colleagues. Those punch cards are emblematic of a time when computers weren't sophisticated enough to understand humans, so humans had to make a disproportionate amount of effort to be understood. Then, as the technology got better, computers took on more and more of the communication burden. That's what happened when punch cards gave way to the command line, then to the graphical user interface, and most recently to the spatial computing unveiled with Apple's new Vision headset.

We can see a similar curve with the ability to accept commands in natural language. We might track the beginning to the 1977 text-based game *Zork*, which could accept a limited set of commands like "go north" or "pick up sword." Then there were early car phone voice commands, where you might say "call Mom," and the car would call anyone from Michael to Monica . . . but not Mom. Then came voice AIs like Alexa and Google Assistant, and all the way up to the Star Trek computer or HAL 9000 (whose "I'm sorry Dave, I'm afraid I can't do that" carries a very different tone from Alexa's "hmmm, I don't know that one").

On that scale, we might plot ChatGPT and its peers as being somewhere between Alexa and Star Trek—smart enough to give you coherent-sounding answers, but not smart enough to ask clarifying questions, or say when it doesn't understand. This introduces a whole new dimension to the "garbage in, garbage out" problem. The phrase applies not only to the training data, but also to the quality of the instructions that you provide. Clear, specific, and detailed instructions will lead to much better responses from the AI.

In AI jargon, the word for instruction is *prompt*. Here are a few examples of prompts from earlier in the book:

Complete the sentence "Mary had a little . . . "

I am a business and marketing coach. What are 10 topics for courses that someone like me could sell?

Let's go with sales and negotiation skills. What are 15 different titles that I could use to call this course?

Outline for me a 6-week curriculum for this course.

Can you write me a script for the first week's lesson?

Please write a 100 word bio of Abraham Lincoln.

Write a bio of Danny Iny.

When you enter a prompt, the AI goes into its trillions of parameters to find the statistically most likely next right words, until you've got your response. But the statistically most likely next right words will depend on how you ask the question.

Case in point: When we were writing the Abraham Lincoln example earlier, the first prompt we gave to ChatGPT was "Please write a short bio of Abraham Lincoln." ChatGPT's answer was 348 words, too long to justify inclusion in a book when it was meant only to illustrate a point. So we tried again: "Please write a 1-paragraph bio of Abraham Lincoln." This yielded a 145-word response. Better, but still too long. So on the third attempt we specified a word count, and got what we were looking for. It was "garbage in, garbage out" in action—bad instructions led to bad results, whereas clear and specific instructions led to much better ones.

That clarity and specificity is even more important with AI than it is with the human assistant of our analogy, because whereas a hardworking, reasonably competent assistant might infer what you're actually looking for from an unclear question, or ask you clarifying questions to help them do the job, AI will just answer the exact question that you asked. That's why "prompt engineering" has become one of the hottest skills of 2023, and there are entire marketplaces where you can pay to buy individual prompts for specific tasks.

But the good news is that while high-quality pre-written prompts can be great time-savers, anyone willing to put in a bit of thoughtfulness and elbow grease can write their own prompts just as well as long as you follow a few basic guidelines:

© marketoonist.com

- **Define the role.** The first trick for getting the best results from an AI is to tell it who it is supposed to be in providing the answer. Start your prompt with "You are a/an" and then fill in the role that you want it to play (like "market researcher," "heart-centered entrepreneur," "stressed-out professional," "HR manager," or whatever else would be helpful).

- **Give parameters for a useful response.** Is there a word count that you're looking for? A format that you'd like the answer to conform to? A framework that should be applied to arrive at the response? A number of examples that you'd like included with the response? The more specific you are about what a good response looks like, the better your odds of getting one.

- **Prime with (prompt for) context.** The more context you can share in advance of actually asking for what you want, the better. And even though the AI has access to its entire database of knowledge, that doesn't mean it's all "top of mind," so to speak. Just as you might get a human assistant in the right headspace with some carefully chosen questions, the same works with AI. For example, you could pose a prompt like "Write a headline for an article about using AI to create online courses," but you might get a better response if you first prime it by asking, "What makes for a really effective article headline?"

- **Stack prompts upon prompts.** One of the innovations of ChatGPT and similar AIs is that you can do more than just ask them a single question—you can conduct an entire conversation. That's what allows for priming with (prompting for) context, as described in the previous bullet. So take advantage of that power by refining and building on past prompts and responses. For example, add something like "This is great, but too long. Can you tighten it up to be about half the length?" or "Can we rewrite it to leave out references to [X]?"

- **Don't hesitate to send it back.** AI offers a number of advantages over the analogous human assistant; for example, it is infinitely faster and cheaper. But another important advantage of AI over a human assistant is that you don't need to manage the AI's morale as it completes tasks. So whereas you might hesitate to tell a human assistant that their work is completely off the mark and needs to be thrown out and redone, with AI there's no reason for such compunctions. If you didn't get what you want, just say so, explain why and how, and ask it to try again.

- **Be polite.** This last point isn't a technical necessity for prompt engineering, but it is important to still be mindful of it. While the technology is advancing at breakneck speed, our programming as human beings is the same as it's been for thousands of years, and our brains just aren't wired to know what artificial intelligence is. That's why we anthropomorphize. Our instinct is to explain our thinking. Many people say "please" and "thank you" to Alexa. And this may seem like a silly artifact of the fact that we aren't used to AI yet, but it isn't. We have to make a conscious decision about how we want to keep interacting with others. If you are curt and callous with AI, it's just a hop, skip, and a jump to being curt with service professionals, and then colleagues at work, and then your family. So my advice, to borrow a phrase from J. M. Barrie, is to "always try to be a little kinder than is necessary." The AI doesn't care, but you should. These tools are powerful, so use them—but don't let them disconnect you from your own humanity.

If you follow these guidelines in crafting your prompts, you'll have a much better chance of getting a really helpful response from the AI.

Always Check the Work!

In the summer of 2019, Danny finally won an almost decade-long negotiation with his wife, and they bought a shiny blue Tesla Model 3. They didn't spring for the full self-driving option (which seemed cool, but not worth $20,000), but it did come equipped with two standard Tesla features: Traffic-Aware Cruise Control, which is like regular cruise control that adjusts speed to keep with traffic and maintain a safe distance from the car ahead; and Lane Assist, which keeps the car steady in the middle of the lane.

So in theory, you could get on the highway, turn on both features, and the car could drive itself for a hundred miles without you ever touching the wheel. But you shouldn't, and the car won't let you. As soon as the features turn on, a dialog pops up with a reminder: "Keep hands on the wheel. Be prepared to take over at any time." And if you do actually take your hands off the wheel, you'll be rebuked by flashing lights and warning chimes (or so we're told—Danny swears he never actually tried this!). In other words, you can treat the car's

AI like a student driver; they can drive as long as a qualified driver is supervising and is ready to intervene if needed.

ChatGPT and its ilk are a very different breed of AI from the technology that powers self-driving cars, but the basic safety guideline is exactly the same: keep your hands on the proverbial wheel, and be prepared to take over at any time. Consider the error-riddled bio that ChatGPT wrote for Danny that we shared a few pages back. If Danny needs a bio of himself, then this is a perfectly good first draft that he can edit and correct, still saving him a bunch of time. His hand would be on the wheel, and he would take control where necessary.

The real issue would be if someone else who isn't intimately familiar with Danny's background and work history asked ChatGPT to write a bio of him. They wouldn't know what corrections need to be made, which means that they wouldn't be able to intervene where appropriate. Consider the analogy that we shared earlier, of AI being to knowledge workers what power tools are to carpenters. For the most part, power tools don't actually enable carpenters to build things that they couldn't before. But they do make it possible for things to be built faster and more easily—so they also require more caution and care since the risk of accident or injury is that much greater!

So, in short, you always have to check the AI's work. Always. You can use AI to research, draft, summarize, or synthesize in areas where you have the expertise to know what they got right and what needs to be revised. But you should *never* count on the AI to discern, decide, finalize, represent, or advise in any area where you don't have the knowledge and expertise to take over.

WORKING WITH AI

Back in his business school days, Danny had a professor who used to say that "all models are wrong, but some are useful." There's a lot of wisdom in those eight words, a reminder in simple terms that the map is not the territory, and we should only use conceptual representations while they serve us. The same applies to the analogy of AI as a hardworking but only reasonably competent human assistant, which is a great tool for internalizing three truths about using AI:

1. Only use AI to do things that you're already capable of and qualified to do.
2. Give it clear and hyper-specific instructions through meticulous prompt engineering.
3. Always check the work that it produces.

But there are also limits to the usefulness of the analogy. Despite what the second letter in AI stands for, it isn't actually intelligent, nor does it have any sort of independence or agency—very much unlike even the least talented human assistant. For that side of things, the power tool analogy works a lot better, in that tools don't do anything *for* you—rather, you do things *with* the assistance of tools. (And similarly, to quote the Geneva Graduate Institute professor of economics Richard Baldwin speaking at the 2023 World Economic Forum's Growth Summit, "AI won't take your job, it's someone using AI that will take your job.")

Thinking of AI as the principal actor is a recipe for disaster, but as long as you stick to using AI as a tool that assists you in doing things that you're already capable of doing, you'll be able to do a lot more of them, and a lot faster. That's why "Did AI write this?" is a misleading question, because a clean "yes" or "no" is only relevant if you're *mis*-using the technology, to do things that you shouldn't be doing in the first place. But if you're using AI responsibly, as per the three bulleted items previously listed, then AI is a tool just like your laptop or Microsoft Word—albeit much more powerful. And in the realm of course creation, this can lead to a lot of leverage. AI can help you:

- Come up with topics and angles for your course
- Gather and synthesize public market insights
- Analyze market research data that you assembled
- Draft marketing assets like sales pages, videos, and emails
- Enhance your offer with time-saving AI shortcuts
- Iterate learning materials to improve student experience
- Draft and develop assignments and worksheets
- Extract and deploy customer feedback and testimonials

In a nutshell, you'll be able to create better courses a lot faster and shorten the gap between you and the marketing of those courses as long as you use AI responsibly. There's just one little problem: There will always be some bad actors who will take advantage of any opportunity to circumvent norms and exploit loopholes. And when it comes to AI, their actions will have a significant impact on the rest of us.

Claim Your Free "Online Courses and AI" Success Bundle

We've created a special bonus resources package to support you in applying the ideas in this book to build and launch your own online course business:

- ✓ **Hybrid Courses Bootcamp video training series**

- ✓ **Audiobook of Danny's bestseller *Effortless***

- ✓ **Library of our most commonly used AI prompts for course building**

This entire resource bundle is our no-cost-whatsoever gift to you.

→GO TO MRSE.CO/GUIDE-RESOURCES TO CLAIM IT!

PART 2:
The Modern
Course Opportunity

CHAPTER 4

The AI Course Apocalypse

"The problem with the race to the bottom is that you might win."
—*Seth Godin*

PICTURE A SHARED OFFICE FRIDGE filled with delicious snacks, which are intended for everyone and paid for with company funds. People are generally responsible and respectful in their snack intake. They take a reasonable amount when they're hungry, and the snacks last awhile; that is, until the day one co-worker starts going hog wild on the communal treats by eating multiple bags of chips and taking two sandwiches instead of one.

At first, you try not to be bothered by it. Maybe they're having a bad day or they're just really hungry. But then, over the next few days, you notice that other co-workers are getting in on the action too. Sally is stuffing her bag with Diet Cokes. Carl's got fistfuls of granola bars. Suddenly, it's a free-for-all, with everyone grabbing more than their fair share.

Before you know it, the snacks are gone. There's nothing left but a few crumbs and some empty wrappers. You're left hungry and disappointed, and so are your colleagues. What happened?

This story of greedy, ravenous co-workers is an example of what economists call a "tragedy of the commons"—a situation where a shared resource is depleted to everyone's detriment because some people act in their individual self-interest and consume more than their fair share. *Commons* can mean a shared grazing field for livestock, but today it usually refers to any shared resource, whether it's air, water, land . . . or the office snacks.

The office fridge is a comparatively lighthearted illustration of this phenomenon, which throughout history has played out in some truly disastrous ways—starting with the original commons, the overgrazing of which was noticed by the eighteenth-century English economist William Forster Lloyd. Farmers acted in their individual self-interest, trying to maximize their own profits, and ended up destroying the commons to everybody's detriment, including their own.

Since then, the tragedy of the commons has been observed in many different contexts, from fishing to air pollution to internet bandwidth. In the early twentieth century, fishermen in the Atlantic Ocean were each trying to catch as many fish as possible, leading to overfishing and a depletion of fish populations. And in the 1960s, factories in the United States were releasing pollutants into the air and water, leading to environmental degradation and health problems. And of course, the pattern continues today. For example, oil companies driven by profits and consumer demand extract and refine oil at a rapid pace, which will eventually deplete the resource altogether—not to mention the harm caused by spills and refinery explosions.

What's true of Big Oil is unfortunately also true of the online courses industry: we can exploit common resources for short-term gain, or we can leverage them for the greater good. When used responsibly, AI has the remarkable potential to change the way we all work, give us new insights, and save a ton of time. But unfortunately, we can't count on everyone to use these AI "commons" responsibly.

MARKETERS. RUIN. EVERYTHING.

We've already established that there's a right way and a wrong way to use AI. The right way is to treat it as an infinitely hardworking and reasonably competent assistant, and the guidelines are simple: give it hyper-specific instructions (a.k.a. prompt engineering) and always check its work.

The wrong way to use AI is to promote it from assistant to expert. This puts you at risk of publishing what AI engineers anthropomorphically refer to as "hallucinations" and "confabulations," and what other people just call "mistakes," "falsehoods," and "things that aren't true." It will still probably *sound* right, but that doesn't mean it actually *is* right.

Most self-respecting experts will act responsibly and use these new technologies with thoughtfulness and integrity. But as Gary Vaynerchuk famously said, "marketers ruin everything," pointing us to the reality that when there's money to be made and a commons to exploit, there will always be someone who rises to the occasion.

There will always be some who won't care much that AI isn't always right; they'll still exploit it to churn out content. It doesn't take a Walt Disney–level imagination to see these dots connect. Consider this hypothetical pitch from the archetypal sleazy internet marketer:

How do you make money? By giving eager buyers what they want.

Where are there eager buyers? Amazon.

And what are they searching for? Everything—including information about really obscure topics that they aren't finding good resources about.

You can help them out! Just search the categories on Amazon and find the niches that don't seem to have good books for people to buy. This is where AI comes in! You don't have to know ANYTHING about the topic, because ChatGPT does! You can have it draft an entire short book on the topic in less than an hour!

How will you know it's good info? You don't—but the reader doesn't either!

And really, you're helping them out, because right now they aren't finding anything at all. So this will be so much better, won't it? Really, you're doing them a huge service, saving them from endless searching! :-P

And . . . scene. This example is hypothetical in that we made it up to illustrate a point, but it's also *not* hypothetical in that we all know that there are people just like this caricature operating in every industry, which is scary and wrong on so many levels. Consider this quick sampling of real headlines for ads and YouTube videos we encountered while writing this book:

"Start monetizing what you know . . . or what ChatGPT knows!"

"Create and sell e-books the lazy way."

"ChatGPT money machine . . . make $1,000+ dollars a day."

"Create e-books in 60 seconds."

"30x in writing output . . . with 0 decrease in work quality."

These are real phrases from marketers looking to use AI the *wrong* way, to make some quick cash. In this sense, the advent of AI tools like ChatGPT has been a sleazy marketer's dream! They can generate content with impressive efficiency, churning out everything from social media posts to online courses to entire articles, or even books, in mere minutes. And with a content-producing machine at your fingertips, the allure for some marketers is undeniable. Why spend hours, or even months, crafting the perfect piece of content when you can have an AI do it in a fraction of the time? Never mind what your actual area of expertise is. Just let AI do the heavy lifting! Give it a few well-chosen prompts, sit back, and let it do all the work. At first, this may seem like a smart move: easy money for almost no work! But the results will be meager and short-lived.

RACING TO THE BOTTOM

Even the most casual comic book fan will recognize the famous dying words of Uncle Ben Parker to his nephew Peter: "With great power comes great responsibility." And compared to the disruptive power of AI, a radioactive spider bite is like a decaf shot of espresso. When marketers abuse the power of digital commons like AI and prioritize profit over quality, things go haywire pretty quickly.

As AI-generated content inevitably floods the online courses industry, we've entered a race to the bottom—the market becomes saturated with low-quality, information-only courses that have been hastily assembled from AI-generated content. As these courses become widespread, valuable knowledge is buried under mountains of digital noise, making it increasingly difficult for learners to find something that's actually accurate and useful.

This "spamification of information" means that learners are bombarded with flashy, AI-generated courses that make big promises but lack substance and depth. And the real injustice is that, as with any tragedy of the commons, the effects won't just be felt by the bad actors who created them. The indiscriminate use of AI will undermine the value and trustworthiness of all content—including yours! With so much low-quality content flooding the market, even the most innovative and informative courses will struggle to stand out and reach their intended audience.

Consider the question that has been posed to content creators with increasing frequency since late 2022: "Did AI write this?" It's not just an idle curiosity, but rather almost an accusation about the work ethic of the creator and quality of whatever is being asked about. And since the bad actors can be expected to be either cagey or dishonest in their responses, it erodes our collective confidence

in all the content that we encounter—from simple articles all the way up to full-blown courses. The industry has already begun to come full circle, with AI tools to create all sorts of content being matched by AI tools to read and condense that same content back down. If you're not going to bother to write it, why should anyone bother reading it?

And we haven't even mentioned pricing, so let's play that part out. Greedy marketers flood the market with quickly produced, information-only courses. Because these courses are so easy to make, they can make a *lot* of them and sell them cheaply. And the abundance of low-cost courses will set a new benchmark for what people are willing to pay for *any* online course. Even honest, expert course creators will feel the pressure to lower their prices.

Then, as students get into the actual content of these cheap courses, they'll realize that many of them are terrible. The quality just isn't up to par, and consumers will feel duped. Trust in the whole online course industry will take a hit, and people will become even more reluctant to invest their time and money in *any* course. And the opportunistic scammers don't even care, because they'll be on to their next grift. It'll be the honorable and ethical course builder (that's you, dear reader!) who is left to pick up the pieces.

That is a pretty bleak picture, but there's good news too. The black cloud of AI-driven disruption has a bright silver lining specifically for legitimate experts who care about making a real difference for their students (that's you again!)—and it all starts with the fact that while a lot is changing (and changing fast), there are some things that will always stay the same.

SHORTCUTS TO TRANSFORMATION

In the roughly three decades since its founding, Amazon has grown to be either *a* or *the* world leader in e-commerce, e-readers, digital cloud services, voice AI assistants, and a lot more. At one point along his journey, Amazon's founder was asked about how he approaches change, given the rapid pace of technological innovation and disruption. He responded by saying:

> *"I very frequently get the question: 'What's going to change in the next 10 years?' And that is a very interesting question; it's a very common one. I almost never get the question: 'What's not going to change in the next 10 years?' And I submit to you that that second question is actually the more important of the two—because you can build a business strategy around the things that are stable in time."*

He went on to explain that while technology and consumer preferences may change rapidly, there are certain fundamental human desires and needs that will never change. Amazon customers will *never* want higher prices, worse customer service, or slower delivery. By focusing on these underlying principles, Bezos believes that businesses can build a strong foundation that will endure even as the specific products or services they offer evolve.

The same principle is true for the online courses industry. It may feel like AI is changing *everything*, and so quickly that it's hard to see what the future holds. But there's something fundamental that is *not* changing, and will never change: what people actually want out of an online course.

No one is will ever say, "Gee, I really wish this course was more generic!" Or, "Boy, I really wish I felt more alone going through this course." Or, most importantly, "I'm improving too quickly! I wish my progress was slower and harder!"

On the contrary, when people join an online course, it's always going to be because they're looking for one thing: transformation. *Transformation* is a word that gets thrown around a lot—so much so that it can start to lose its meaning. So what do we mean by *transformation*? You might think about it as a shift in feelings: Your students feel one way before your course, and they feel another way (better) after they finish the course. And their feelings shift because they understand something differently, or they can do something better than they could before.

For example, a new coach might feel frustrated, incompetent, or embarrassed because they're not getting any clients, so they go through an online course about client attraction, and they learn how to land their first clients. They come away knowing a process that they can successfully implement. Now, instead of the negative feelings they started with, they might feel confident, hopeful, or relieved. The course transformed what they know, what they're able to do, and how they feel.

People want a transformation, but they also want it as quickly and painlessly as possible—they want a *shortcut*. That's our second key term. And we don't mean *shortcut* in a bad sense of trying to shortchange a process, but rather in the very legitimate sense that if you have the expertise and experience to know how to get something done, you'll be able to do it faster, more easily, and more reliably than someone who isn't as well trained.

That's the silver lining: that people will always want transformation and will always value a shortcut that allows them to get it in less time, at less cost, and with less risk of failure than if they were to make the attempt without your help.

Our new coach from the previous example might have spent months and months spinning their wheels trying to figure out how to attract clients. They'd spend time down internet rabbit holes, or on attracting clients through trial and error—and mostly error! They'd spend money on ineffective trainings. And all that added up to a lot of energy spent, and largely wasted.

But then they find your course, which leverages your legitimate expertise in the area of client attraction to tell them just what they need to know and exactly how to do it. What you teach really works, and it works quickly. That's what people are really looking for when they invest in an online course: not a bunch of AI-generated text, but a real transformation, delivered efficiently. If you can deliver that sort of transformation—and your prospects have good reason to trust you when you say that this is the case—then you will be perfectly poised to thrive with online courses, even after the AI course apocalypse.

CHAPTER 5

Engineering Transformation

"Tell me and I forget. Teach me and I remember. Involve me and I learn."

—Benjamin Franklin

THE CATCHPHRASE "wax on, wax off" has become synonymous with karate instruction and learning by doing. It comes from the 1984 movie *The Karate Kid*, about a scrawny kid from New Jersey named Daniel LaRusso. He moves to California and runs afoul of a group of boys who study a predatory brand of karate called Cobra Kai, whose motto is "Strike first, strike hard, no mercy."

In desperation, LaRusso cracks open an old book about karate and tries to teach himself the martial art by practicing kicks in the air. Unsurprisingly, he isn't successful, and his next several encounters with the bullies go decidedly in their favor. LaRusso is finally rescued by Mr. Miyagi, a wise old Japanese handyman who teaches the boy his own brand of karate, which emphasizes self-defense and inner balance.

The training is nontraditional. While his Cobra Kai rivals practice punching and kicking in their dojo, Mr. Miyagi demands no-questions-asked obedience, and assigns LaRusso to tasks like sanding the floor, painting the fence, and waxing his cars (hence the iconic "wax on, wax off"). LaRusso's patience with seemingly pointless manual labor wears thin, and he challenges Mr. Miyagi to stop wasting his time. It all comes to a head in the scene where Mr. Miyagi unleashes a flurry of punches and kicks that LaRusso blocks, surprising himself by using the movements he had practiced for sanding the floor, painting the fence, and so on.

It's one of the movie's classic moments, marking the start of LaRusso's transformation from a wimpy, anxious kid to a competent, capable karateka who has found his center. And while creative license has obviously been taken in illustrating the process of learning karate, there are still some profound lessons for us about the arts of teaching and learning.

For one, the movie strongly makes the point that we do in fact need teachers—trying to figure something out on your own is by far the slowest and most painful way to learn. But it takes more than just a teacher (or set of videos) sharing even the most insightful and compelling information. Learners need a process that allows them to practice the skills they're working to master, and to receive nuanced and helpful feedback that supports their improvement. And now more than ever, it's not just that students need these elements to succeed; they also need to see that these elements are all present in order to be willing to buy in the first place.

In this chapter we'll unpack the different ingredients of transformation, starting with the most foundational one of all: legitimate expertise.

LEGITIMATE EXPERTISE

Imagine you're catching up with a friend about what's been going on in your lives. You mention that you've been feeling a little blah lately.

Your friend immediately jumps in to tell you that you have depression and need to get medication to treat it. You say, "Maybe, but I think I just need more sleep! My partner's snoring has gotten worse." Your friend digs in: "No, it's definitely depression. Difficulty sleeping is a classic sign!" You stare at her for a minute. "What?" she says. "I just finished a great book on psychology! Your symptoms are plain as day!"

Does your friend know a little bit about psychology after reading this book? Perhaps. But should she be diagnosing you? Obviously not. There's a common trope that reading a few books on a subject will make you a de facto expert on that topic. And it is true that you'd have more knowledge about that subject than most everyday people. But simply learning information is not what makes an expert. At best, it makes you an armchair expert, with a level of confidence that isn't justified by your actual understanding of the subject matter.

Armchair experts equipped with AI are becoming more and more of a nuisance to the online courses industry, as we saw in the previous chapter. Cheap, information-only courses (with no guarantee that the information is even correct) will flood the market and drive prices way down.

You'll differentiate yourself with *legitimate*, not armchair, expertise, which requires not only knowledge, but also real-world experience and insight. And legitimate expertise doesn't just mean that you know something (or even a lot) about a subject, as ChatGPT appears to. True expertise is marked not simply by knowledge but also by insight, a unique perspective or observation that challenges commonly held assumptions. In fact, we like to use a quick formula to think about expertise:

"Most people think X, but actually it's Y."

An example of a real expert would be renowned primatologist Jane Goodall. Goodall embarked in 1960 on a groundbreaking mission to study chimpanzees in their natural habitat, and her approach to studying chimpanzees was highly unconventional for its time. Rather than confining the animals to a laboratory and subjecting them to experiments, she chose to observe them in the wild, tracking their movements, recording their interactions, and gaining a deep understanding of their social dynamics.

Through years of meticulous fieldwork, Goodall gained unique insights into the behavior of chimpanzees that challenged conventional wisdom. Her discovery that chimpanzees have distinct personalities and use tools like sticks and rocks to obtain food shocked the scientific community and overturned long-standing beliefs about the capabilities of nonhuman animals.

Goodall's groundbreaking research has had a profound impact on our understanding of animal intelligence, communication, and social behavior. Her work has inspired a new generation of scientists to study animal behavior and ecology in the wild, and it continues to be a source of inspiration for those dedicated to protecting the planet's biodiversity.

So, what makes Goodall a legitimate expert? Has she read (more than) a few books about primates? Presumably. But reading is not the source of her expertise. She spent decades in the field, even living among chimpanzees, to experience firsthand what their lives were like. That is how she gained unique insights into their capabilities and behavior.

Going back to our "most people think X, but actually it's Y" formulation of expertise, an expert like Jane Goodall might say that "most people think tool use sets humans apart from other apes, but I've observed chimpanzees creating and using tools to get food and use as toys." Or she might reflect on the research process itself, saying that "most people think primatologists should study animals from afar, but you learn so much more by immersing yourself in their lives."

Real expertise isn't about the ability to regurgitate commonly held knowledge about your field. Rather, legitimate expertise is about knowing the boundary conditions of where those commonly held ideas should stop applying, and where most people approaching your industry have got it wrong.

To further illustrate this concept, we asked ChatGPT to give us a few more examples of real experts and their "everyone thinks X but actually it's Y" thinking, and here's what we got:

Marie Curie: Most people think that elements are static and cannot be changed, but through my research on radioactivity, I discovered that some elements, like radium and polonium, actually break down and transform into other elements over time.

Warren Buffett: Most people think that the key to successful investing is constantly chasing the latest hot stocks or market trends, but it's actually about adhering to a disciplined, long-term, value-based investment strategy.

Muhammad Yunus: Most people think that poor people are not creditworthy and cannot be trusted to repay loans, but through the creation of microcredit and the Grameen Bank, I've demonstrated that low-income individuals are reliable borrowers and can use small loans to escape poverty.

Brené Brown: Most people think vulnerability is a sign of weakness, but my research has shown that embracing vulnerability is actually essential for building resilience, connection, and personal growth.

Wangari Maathai: Most people think that environmental conservation and economic development are at odds, but my work with the Green Belt Movement demonstrates that empowering communities to plant trees and restore their environments can create jobs and improve living conditions.

And of course, we can share illustrations from the world of on-line courses too. If you were to ask Danny, who is recognized as an expert in the online courses industry, he might say any number of things about online courses, including that . . .

> . . . most people think online courses are about the trans-mission of information, but they're actually about creating transformation through transformative learning journeys.

Or that . . .

> . . . most people think you need to fully create your online course before you sell it, but you should actually create it together with your students in a pilot program, after you sell it.

Or even that . . .

> . . . too many people think online courses are about creat-ing passive income, but they're actually much better for creating financial leverage and scaling impact.

For you to succeed with online courses in a post-AI world, it's not enough to know the same stuff that most other experts know—you also need the insight and perspective to know where most others are wrong, and what should be done differently. Of course, it's not enough for that knowledge to just exist in your head. To thrive as an online course creator, you'll also need to create a learning journey that reliably engineers that transformation for your students.

THE MASTERY LEARNING JOURNEY

One of the most influential educational theorists of the last century was Benjamin Bloom. He gave us many useful ideas, including his famous taxonomy of effective learning, which informs curriculum designers to this day. He also created the concept of mastery learning, which is of particular importance to online course creators on a mission to engineer real transformation.

To understand what it's all about, consider an analogy that we first heard from Khan Academy founder Sal Khan. Let's pretend, Khan suggests, that educating a child is like building a house. You'll start by building the foundation. Then on top of that comes the first floor. Then the electrical and plumbing infrastructure. Then the second floor, and so on. Now let's imagine that after each step, the work gets inspected. And let's say, for example, that after the foundation is built, the inspection comes back with a report that shows the foundation is about 70% complete.

So the moment of truth: Do you keep on building on top of a 70% complete foundation, or do you go back and finish the last 30% before moving on? Ethical builders, regulating bodies, and anyone who might one day live in the house would all insist on going back and fixing the foundation before moving on to the next step.

And that, in a nutshell, is what mastery learning is all about: the completely obvious yet at the same time still revolutionary idea that you shouldn't move on to lesson two until you've mastered lesson one. It would seem to be common sense, but it also happens to be supported as a best practice by numerous studies, starting with research that Bloom himself conducted as far back as 1984. He compared three classes of students:

CONTROL GROUP: Regular lecture-based classroom

VARIATION A: Lecture-based classroom that followed a mastery learning approach

VARIATION B: Mastery learning approach + one-on-one tutoring for students

The results of the study were staggering: variation A performed a full standard deviation above the control, and variation B performed two standard deviations above the control. In case your statistical analysis skills are a bit rusty, here's a translation to plain English, in Bloom's own words: "the average tutored student was above 98 percent of the students in the control class."

At its core, the process of mastery learning isn't all that complicated. There are just three steps that students need to go through in order to achieve real learning: first consuming new information, then applying it themselves, and finally getting useful feedback that allows them to improve their understanding.

CONSUME   **APPLY**   **IMPROVE**

Courses that effectively take students though each of these three steps are the ones that deliver real transformation, which isn't all that surprising. We intuitively understand that learning takes more than just passively consuming information. Whether you're teaching dog obedience, tax exemptions, or child development, your students will need to do the (often difficult) work of implementing what you're teaching. Along the way they might need some clarification or specific advice about a particular situation, and they'll definitely need meaningful feedback about what they're doing well and what needs to change and improve.

Step 1: Tell Me Something I Don't Know (Consume)

The first step in the mastery learning journey is the one that is most immediately familiar to most aspiring course creators: the consumption of new information. This can be through a live lecture, pre-recorded video, text essay, or whatever other media might fit the situation. But that takes us only so far, because of a fundamental reality of how learning works: Learning about something doesn't automatically translate to the ability to actually do what we're learning. In other words, we don't get good at things just from watching videos or reading explanations. To develop any sort of meaningful competence, we have to apply what we're learning.

Step 2: Let Me Try It Myself (Apply)

The second step in the mastery learning journey is application, where you take what you're learning and do something with it. Application can be theoretical (e.g., exercises and worksheets) or practical (e.g., actually doing things in your business or life). Only when we begin to apply what we're learning do we get a sense of how much we really do, or don't, understand. And only by applying can there be an opportunity for us to receive any sort of meaningful feedback.

Step 3: Give Me Helpful Feedback (Improve)

The third step in the mastery learning journey is to improve with the assistance of helpful and nuanced feedback. This is the crucial ingredient that leads to meaningful improvement for the student, which is notably absent from the AI-generated sameness that floods most markets. Only courses that offer opportunities for the students to apply what they've learned and receive corrective feedback will be exempt from the AI-induced race to the bottom—because of the value that they create, and also because they include components that clearly stand out to prospective students.

CHAPTER 6
The Hybrid Course Revolution

"The idea is to go from numbers to information to understanding."

—Hans Rosling

IN EARLY 2005, Michael and Lily Idov opened a small café on New York's Lower East Side. They sold Vienna roast from Vienna, which is lighter and sweeter than bitter Italian espresso, so you don't have to drown it in milk. And the coffee was served on silver trays with a glass of water and a little chocolate cookie. It was a charming concept . . . and six months later it was out of business. This wasn't a function of poor management—in Michael's own words, it was an "inevitability."

It all comes down to the math. When you figure the cost of rent and labor against the value of a sale times the twenty to twenty-five people that a "cozy" café can hold, you arrive at an inescapably money-losing proposition. There are two common ways to get around the math: you can augment your sales with people who take their coffee to go, or the proprietors can save on the labor costs by doing all the work themselves. Which isn't a real solution, because there's only so long that a business can be subsidized by the unpaid labor of its employers.

The Idovs had to learn the same lesson as every other entre-preneur (hopefully before running out of money): that you have to understand which business you're actually in. Sure, you could say that the Idovs were in the coffee business, in the same way that Starbucks, Nespresso, and Lavazza are all in the coffee business. But if you want to be successful, a little more nuance goes a long way. And understanding which business you're in means understanding the underlying math that will drive its success (or failure).

THE BUSINESS MATH OF ONLINE COURSES

Over the past decade, we've supported thousands of coaches, consultants, authors, speakers, and experts on their journeys from online course pre-contemplation to action and success. In some ways, they end up exactly where they imagined; they really do impact more people, make more money, and feel more free. But in other ways, they discover that their guesses were woefully uneducated. The imagined picture usually looks something like this:

> *I'll take my book or keynote presentation and create a "course version" of the same content. Then I'll set it up online, and people will buy it—that's my ticket to (limitless!) passive income.*

There was a time, in the early days of online courses, when this was (somewhat) doable. But not anymore—and not just because turning a book or keynote presentation into a course generally makes for a pretty bad course (more on that later). The challenge runs deeper, to a fundamental contradiction between the vision of passive income and the reality of most aspiring course entrepreneurs.

That's because, for most people, the words *passive income* conjure up a vague picture of

1. strangers on the internet "automagically" discovering something you've built, then
2. finding your message compelling enough to pull out their credit cards, and then
3. getting everything that they paid for . . .

. . . all without you having to lift a finger, or maybe even be awake! (There's an alluring mystique to the idea of "making money while you sleep"!) And sure, you might have to work hard to build the perpetual money machine, but once it's built you can just "set it and forget it"—or so the fantasy goes. But in real life, it doesn't usually work that way, because real passive income requires that two very particular stars need to align, which aren't often seen together: low price and high volume.

PASSIVE INCOME = LOW PRICE × HIGH VOLUME

Low price is necessary because if the price is high, neither the sale nor the fulfillment can be passive. On the sales side, over a certain price threshold the cycles become more complex and often require the intervention of a salesperson. And on the fulfillment side, the more people pay, the more they expect to receive, such as support, interactivity, and coaching. Now, there's nothing wrong with any of that, and there are great businesses to be built that include a more involved sales process and coaching of customers once they buy, but while they can be rewarding and lucrative, they don't usually fit the image conjured up by the word *passive*. So passive income requires a low price.

But a low price isn't enough; it also requires high volume, because if the price is low and you want the income to add up to a meaningful amount, you need to make up for that low price with high volume—low price times low volume might be passive, but it won't be much income! So we also need high volume—in other words, we need to sell a whole lot of courses! But that is often easier said than done, and to understand why, we need to take a short digression into the world of unit economics.

Unit Economics: Why Passive Income Is (Probably) a Fantasy

Unit economics are the nuts and bolts of what makes businesses successful. If you've ever tried to raise money from investors—or even if you like to watch shows like *Shark Tank* or listen to podcasts like *The Pitch*—you know that a charismatic founder's cool idea is just the beginning. Once you've got their attention, they'll want to dig deeper.

The first thing investors want to understand is your *contribution profit*. To find that, we start with the price of whatever it is you're selling, and take away both the cost of acquiring the customer (i.e., direct sales and marketing costs) and the cost of fulfilling the sale (i.e., materials, shipping, and support). Your contribution profit is whatever amount is left over after those "variable costs" are taken out.

Now take that contribution profit and multiply it by all the sales you make. If you get a number that is smaller than all your "fixed costs" (like rent and salaries), you're in trouble—that's what happened to Michael and Lily Idov's café, simply because they couldn't serve the volume of customers that they would have needed to turn a profit. If it's more or less on par, you'll live to fight another day. And if you have a lot of money left over, that means you've got a great business.

(Some Silicon Valley investors like to believe that unit economics aren't that important in the early stages of a company's growth, and sometimes they're right, but it's only a matter of time before the math catches up to you.)

In the context of an online course business, a good rule of thumb is that for the math to work, the price of your course will split into three more or less equal parts: one-third customer acquisition, one-third fulfillment, and one-third contribution profit. So if you sell a $999 course, you can afford to spend about $333 to attract and enroll the student, $333 to deliver a great experience, and you'll have $333 left over to contribute to all your other regular expenses.

Contribution Profit   Fullfillment   Customer Acquisition

Now that we know what unit economics are, we can talk about why they make the passive income fantasy out of reach for most course entrepreneurs. Remember that passive income requires two things: low price (otherwise it isn't passive) and high volume (otherwise it isn't much income). But we're also constrained by unit economics, with a rule of thumb that we can spend about a third of the retail price (which is already low) on acquiring the customer. And a third of a low price is very little money. And customers are usually expensive to acquire. Here's how you figure out the number for you:

1. How many leads do you need to get your message in front of to get one sale?
2. How much does it cost (in dollars, or value of time) to attract one lead?

Multiply the answers to both questions, and you get your customer acquisition cost (CAC). So, for example, if you run ads on Facebook and it costs you $5 to get a lead (which is on the low end of reasonable), and your regular process converts one out of every 50 leads into a customer (which is probably optimistic), then this is the math:

$$\$5/lead \times 50\ leads = \$250\ customer\ acquisition\ cost$$

And if you can spend roughly a third of your retail price to acquire a customer, then that means you'd need to charge $750 to make the math work on those Facebook ads—which is probably more than you can charge and still have the experience be completely passive. So that doesn't work. The only way you can make the passive income dream a reality is if you can find an unusually cheap way of attracting students. And there *are* ways of attracting students very inexpensively, which is why passive income isn't a total myth. But unfortunately, most of those ways are unattainable for most course creators.

Unusually Affordable Ways of Attracting Traffic

Early mover advantage. Early movers on the right opportunities get a whole lot of advantages. If we're talking markets (e.g., you teach the first internet course on weight loss), then you get in before anyone is there to compete. If we're talking platforms (e.g., you were on Facebook or Instagram or TikTok before anybody else), then it's easier to build your following and your ads run for cheap. The problem is that these days, most markets are mature, and your only shot at being an early mover is to take a chance on the social media world's hot flavor of the week (the hot new trend could be a rising star like TikTok, but it could also be a wave that quickly crashes, like Periscope or Clubhouse).

Prime placement. There are places where loads of your ideal prospects are already hanging out, like the top of the search platforms like Google, YouTube, and Amazon, or the home pages of course marketplaces like Udemy, Highbrow, or Skillshare. If you have the connections or positioning to land one of those coveted spots, it will very inexpensively expose loads of new leads to your message and offer. Unfortunately, there are far more people vying to secure those spots than there are spots to be had, so it's pretty competitive.

Celebrity status. Being a celebrity—whether A-list globally, or B-list in your own industry—makes everything easier. You're more likely to get the prime placements on platform sites because they want to showcase their association with you. Your ad costs go down because people are more likely to want to know what you're up to. Oh, and you've very likely amassed an audience of tens or hundreds of thousands of people. That's the Kylie Cosmetics success plan—going from zero to a billion dollars in five years with twelve employees and no marketing budget, thanks to Kylie Jenner's 141 million followers.

Buying in bulk. There's a dirty little secret that advertising gurus don't like to tell you when they promise that "you too can turn $1 into $10 by following our system"—that the prices they pay for ads and the prices you pay for ads aren't the same, because they're buying in bulk. Yes, they might be buying leads on Facebook for just a few dollars, but that's because they're buying thousands of them every day. If you're just dipping your toe in the water (which Facebook and other ad platforms and media companies loosely define as spending less than six figures annually), they'll charge you a multiple of that price.

Subsidized acquisition. Remember how I said that you can spend about a third of your list price to acquire the customer? Well, there's an exception to that rule, in cases where the money will come from somewhere else—either you just have very deep pockets (like Masterclass after they raised $100 million dollars of venture capital), or there is a back end to your business whereby once you acquire a customer, you know they'll buy more stuff from you. Let's say, for example, that in addition to your $300 course, you also sell a $30,000 mastermind, and experience has shown you that roughly one out of every hundred course buyers will upgrade to the next level. In that case, you can afford to spend twice as much to acquire the customer (a third of the course price, plus a third of a hundredth of the mastermind price).

So yes, if you blew up on Facebook before it was cool, control the top search rankings on Google and YouTube, have major celebrity status and a hundred thousand raving fans, can afford to buy traffic in bulk, or can overspend on marketing because you know you'll make it up on the back end . . . sure, adding some passive income to your business is no big deal. But that doesn't describe the reality of most course creators. And contrary to popular belief, this underlying math doesn't change because of AI—or at least not the way that most people think.

But . . . What About AI?

Now that we have a few hundred repetitions under our belts of teaching the concepts of this chapter, we know that they can be both clear and confounding . . . at the same time!

Clear, because the math isn't all that complicated; the retail price of your course splits three ways between the customer acquisition, fulfillment, and contribution profit—which also means that you can't build a sustainable business charging a price so low that you can't afford to acquire new customers, unless you have an unfair advantage that allows you to acquire customers at less cost than most of your competitors.

But at the same time confounding, because . . . AI! After all, if you have an untiring and infinitely hardworking digital assistant that doesn't need to be paid overtime, or even a salary—how could that *not* change the math? And the instinct there is correct—AI absolutely does change the math, just not the way most people expect.

Let's go back to our three-way split of the retail price of your course. Where does AI fit in? AI doesn't reduce the costs of fulfillment; whatever materials or support you'd want to provide will still be required. Nor does AI change the cost to acquire a customer—whatever marketing and sales processes you were going to engage in still need to happen.

AI does matter, but on the other side of the equation: in the production and deployment of new courses. The productivity gains of AI mean that you can test, develop, and deploy courses much, much faster—and you'll see exactly how to apply the tools to do that in later chapters. But it doesn't change the fundamental business math; if passive income was out of your reach before AI, it's still out of your reach now that AI is part of your tool kit.

Marketing and the Red Queen

There is one exception to the "no impact of AI" idea, which is where the marketing processes involve labor that can be replaced by AI. But this doesn't actually reduce the cost, because of something called the Red Queen Effect. You can Google the concept, but it basically plays out like this:

1. An enterprising marketer starts using AI (responsibly) to augment their human talent, such as in the writing of content for search engine optimization.

2. This cuts the time to create high-quality content in half. Score!

3. The marketer still has a full-time SEO writer on staff, so she puts them to good use, doubling their SEO output.

4. Twice as much SEO content means twice the results, and the company surges ahead in the rankings. Double score!

5. But this advantage is short-lived. Pretty soon all their competitors are using AI to see the same productivity benefits too. (The ones that don't keep losing ground, until they're out of business.)

6. With everyone using these AI technologies to double their productivity, the industry-wide amount of SEO content grows dramatically.

7. The search engines still have a finite amount of space on their results pages, so they make it harder to rank.

8. The market finds a new equilibrium; everybody spends roughly the same amount and gets roughly the same results (by producing more content—but that doesn't really matter).

And if you're wondering whether this can be avoided if everyone just uses AI to increase productivity without increasing their total output, we'll refer you to the section in the previous chapter about the tragedy of the commons.

That means you'll have to settle for the practical alternative. With the passive income formula of low price multiplied by high volume off the table, you must go the opposite way, toward a business model driven by premium courses, priced high enough to require only a small volume of sales.

FROM SAGE ON THE STAGE TO GUIDE ON THE SIDE

In 1981, the world was introduced to Harrison Ford's archetype of an archaeologist, in the form of the fedora-wearing, whip-wielding Indiana Jones. The film captured imaginations, and according to *National Geographic*, some of the best archaeologists in the world today say that their interest in the field was sparked by the exciting career of Dr. Jones. There's just one little problem: the Indiana Jones image of archaeology couldn't be further from the truth. Most archaeologists spend their time meticulously digging and cataloging findings, conducting laboratory analyses, writing reports, and applying for grants (the job often involves more paperwork than treasure hunting).

This phenomenon isn't relegated to the world of archaeology. Across many fields, there is often a wide gap between the first glamorous exposure that sparks interests and captures imaginations and the actual experience of doing the job. For medical professionals, routine care, paperwork, and emotional demands often overshadow the glamour and intensity shown on *ER* or *House, M.D.* Legal work involves a lot more research, documentation, and compliance tasks than you might expect from watching *The Practice* or *Suits*. And good policing is much more about paperwork, routine patrols, and community outreach than you might expect from watching *The Rookie* or *Brooklyn Nine-Nine*.

And the same is true for the business of online courses. From the outside, people tend to imagine it as being about creating a series of videos that you can set and forget inside of a membership site, connected to a funnel that "automagically" drives sales so you can earn passive income. But as we've seen, that's not usually how it works in real life. Of course, just as lawyers do occasionally give impassioned speeches in high-profile cases and cops do occasionally engage in high-speed, high-stakes chases, there are edge cases where the paradigm of the sage on the stage uses digital technology to broadcast their message to millions of people, making a mint in the process. But those edge cases are rare; as we've seen, most people don't have the celebrity, reach, or resources to make that model work, and that's a good thing, because that setup doesn't lead to much impact for the students anyway.

But the opportunity for modern experts is attractive in its own right: to be the sort of instructor better described as the guide on the side—the one who creates an experience rich enough to take students through all three steps of the mastery learning journey, and who reliably engineers transformation. That leads to much better outcomes, for both the students (who get the transformation that they're really after) and for the course creator (who enjoys the leverage, freedom, and impact afforded by a premium online course).

There's a name for this sort: *hybrid*. Hybrid courses have a double advantage in that they're able to deliver a transformation that is actually worth paying for. And in the race-to-the-bottom era of the AI course apocalypse, they're also easier to sell—because customers can see that they are obviously different from the sort of courses that AI can easily spit out.

The Wide World of Hybrid

In the vast majority of disciplines, making binary decisions just reduces what is possible and corners you into a way of working that isn't quite as effective as you'd like. When you start combining different things, the whole becomes greater than the sum of its parts.

Take cooking, for example—sure, at times all you want is a single flavor, but the really delicious and memorable meals most often come from adding all sorts of different spices to a dish. Imagine if the only spice you could use was salt! Some things would be great, but others would be seriously lacking.

Or take music—the world would be much poorer if we could play only one note, or if we could only ever listen to one instrument at a time. We think it's fair to say that a lot of amazing creations would have been missed out on if we constrained ourselves to just the binary of either piano or cello.

Let's use a more pertinent example—what if you could use only one medium to teach? Only audio, or only text? Would it be possible to get your ideas across? Sure—look, you're learning what our thoughts are just through text! But the fact that it can "kinda sorta" work doesn't mean that we need to, or even should, limit ourselves.

So what are the different hybrid options we have in front of us? Here are just some examples of dimensions on which you can move the lever from one extreme to somewhere in the middle:

- **Curriculum vs. Coaching.** We've already talked about this, but it still has to make the list. Do you take your students through a predetermined set of cookie-cutter steps, or do you create a custom-tailored experience that is unique to them? Instead of choosing one or the other, you can get the best of both worlds by creating a curriculum of the common steps and concepts that people need to take and master, and then supplementing it with support and coaching at the points where they will need customized direction and guidance.

- **Recorded vs. Live.** Should you pre-record your lesson content for people to go through whenever they want, or deliver everything live? Again, you don't have to choose one or the other. Get the best of both worlds with a "flipped classroom" structure, whereby they get the lesson materials pre-recorded, and workshopping or Q&A can happen live.

- **On-Demand vs. On A Schedule.** Would it be better for your students to access your materials and go through the program whenever they feel like it (even if that means never!) or on a schedule that you set? You can blend these two options by having a cohort-based experience with a fixed start and end date, but have it include ranges of times for things to get done, and let your students retain access to the lesson materials (and some degree of support) for an extended period of time afterward.

- **Solo vs. Community.** Will it work best for people to go through the program completely on their own, or do it as part of a community? Instead of making a blanket decision for all of your students, why not create degrees of freedom and choice by having a solo experience with add-on components of community interaction and facilitation, either as a cohort or as a global community for the entire program?

- **Virtual vs. In-Person.** Should people access your materials online from their devices, or should they come to meet you for an immersive, in-person experience? You can merge these two options (and get the best of both worlds) by delivering your core program virtually, and having an add-on in-person component at key points in the program. The in-person component can be at an extra charge, included as part of their base tuition, or offered as a bonus for doing the work in your program.

The point here isn't that *everything* has to be hybrid, but rather that these are all dimensions with which you can adjust the lever in either direction, based on whatever will work best for the transformation and experience that you want to deliver to your students— because that's what this is all about: delivering a transformation so valuable to your students that they will be willing and eager to pay, engage, and evangelize after the fact. That is the real engine of online course business success, and when you build that engine, the results can be spectacular.

Claim Your Free "Online Courses and AI" Success Bundle

We've created a special bonus resources package to support you in applying the ideas in this book to build and launch your own online course business:

✓ **Hybrid Courses Bootcamp video training series**

✓ **Audiobook of Danny's bestseller *Effortless***

✓ **Library of our most commonly used AI prompts for course building**

This entire resource bundle is our no-cost-whatsoever gift to you.

→**GO TO MRSE.CO/GUIDE-RESOURCES TO CLAIM IT!**

PART 3:
Your First Hybrid Course

ONLINE COURSES CHANGED Danny's life; first, as a student, he learned the skills to begin growing his business; and then, as an instructor, he was able to create leverage, freedom, and impact in his business and life—and a big part of that leverage was hiring the rest of us! But here's the secret that some people don't know about Danny's mostly up-and-to-the-right business trajectory: his very first online course he created didn't do well at all.

It started with a brilliant idea . . . one that he was sure would be a huge hit. He went into his "bat cave" and spent substantial amounts of time, money, and energy putting the course together. He kept tweaking and improving it, trying to make it absolutely perfect. Finally, the big day arrived, and he launched it to the world—certain it would make a huge impact, and earn a lot of money in the process. But the sales never came. To say that it was a giant disappointment would be an understatement; Danny had literally spent thousands of hours before making a cent, and in the entire lifetime of that course it didn't sell so many as fifty copies.

Danny learned from the experience and never made that mistake again. The next three courses that he launched were all blockbuster successes—proving that the learning experience, while painful, was absolutely worthwhile. With the first of those three courses, which he launched in 2012, it took only 60 hours of work to go from start to first dollar earned. With the second (launched in 2013), it took only 30 hours, and with the third (launched in 2015), it took only 20 hours. And it's not just about speed to market, either—the quality of the courses kept getting better!

What Danny learned through hard experience—and what we now teach the coaches, consultants, speakers, authors, and experts that our company trains—is that we can't help but approach course building (like any new endeavor) with a set of assumptions, such as what exactly people want to pay to learn from you, what prior knowledge they'll bring to the table, what they'll find most challenging, and what the best way will be to get each point across. And some of those assumptions are bound to be wrong. In some cases (because of inexperience or sheer bad luck), the majority of your assumptions turn out to be wrong. And in other cases (when you have a lot of experience teaching about your topic and working with your target audience), only a small portion of the assumptions turn out to be wrong.

The trouble is that building a successful online course business is more like building a bridge than writing a paper. If you get 90% of the work right on a paper for school, you'll get an A, but if you get 90% of the work right when building a bridge, you'll get a lawsuit. So even if your assumptions are off by as little as 10–20%, it's a problem. And there's no way of knowing in advance which 10–20% of your assumptions will turn out to be the wrong ones.

The only way to know for sure is to test. Your first course, which we call a "pilot" course, should be designed to validate a few basic assumptions as quickly and inexpensively as possible—quickly so that you can pivot and iterate rapidly if the situation calls for it, and inexpensively so that you minimize the risk to the entrepreneur. It's the Silicon Valley dictum of "first make it work, then make it better."

Neither of these goals—speed and low cost—are met by the ambitions of most first-time course creators, who tend to want to teach everything about everything that relates to their topic area and wind up with plans for a massive six-month or yearlong course. That sort of course takes ages to produce, which means a very long timeline to gaining real knowledge about whether the market actually wants it. Adding insult to injury, the broad focus of such a mega-course means that while it's somewhat valuable to a lot of people, it isn't very valuable to anyone, which makes it very hard to sell. And if the course does somehow attract students, and those students struggle to get to the finish line (which is very likely on the first iteration of any course), the expansive scope makes it very difficult to diagnose what exactly went wrong—nor is it easy to discover what can be done differently or better in the future.

To avoid all that, and set ourselves up to learn the lessons we need in time to inform future decisions, we start with a pilot. This isn't the final, extended magnum opus that you might one day create. Rather, it's the minimum viable version for you to get outside validation that you're on the right track. And through it you can validate demand for the course you want to offer, and co-create a transformative learning experience that is worth paying for.

The primary goal for launching your pilot is to validate demand for your offer. When you enter a new space or try to build something for the first time, your priority should be to gather information—to validate that people are willing and eager to pay for what you want to do, in the format that you want to provide. In other words, you need to find out if people actually *want* what you're selling. This validation happens in stages, culminating with the pilot itself, and will help you avoid wasted effort. And, as a bonus, pilot courses are actually *easier* to sell!

In this next (and longest) part of the book, we will walk you through the process that we've developed, refined, and taught to thousands of course creators over the years. And along the way we'll share some notes about how to leverage AI, but we encourage you to make your own notes about where and how AI might be able to help.

CHAPTER 7

Match Market
and Transformation

*"We fit together like custom pieces from a two person puzzle.
And therefore, you are exactly my perfect kind of nice."*
                                                    —*Penny Reid*

AS DANNY WROTE in his book *Effortless*, the *Salvator Mundi* is an
obscure painting thought to be a later work of the Renaissance artist
Leonardo da Vinci. There is some controversy around its authentic-
ity (not all experts agree that it was actually painted by Leonardo)
and the numerous conservation and cleaning efforts that it under-
went. Despite these questions, the painting was sold at auction on
November 15, 2017, for an astronomical sum of $450.3 million USD.

The auction price tag makes the *Salvator Mundi* the most expensive painting ever sold to this day. But does that make it the best?
Hardly. We think you'd be hard-pressed to even make the case that
it's the best painting by Leonardo da Vinci! Consider, for example,
the approachable beauty of his first version of *The Virgin of the Rocks*,
the inspiring possibilities suggested by his *Vitruvian Man*, the mys-
terious smile of the *Mona Lisa*, or the piercing self-awareness of his
Turin Self-Portrait.

You could make a good argument for why any of these pieces
are the best, but it's not a debate that can ever be won. Fundamentally,
whether a painting is the best or most beautiful is true only in the eye

of the beholder. In the same way, your course can only ever exist in relation to the needs and wants of a particular student.

This isn't about having the "right" answer, the "best" marketing, or the "most clever" funnel—because none of those things actually exist! It's about aligning everything you do with your ideal student. In other words, *matching* your ideal student to your offering. The more closely aligned you are with your student's desires, the easier it will be to create your course empire. So before we can talk about how to design your course and enroll students, we have to get crystal clear about who those students are.

YOUR TARGET STUDENT

If you've ever tried online dating, you'll know that when you join, most platforms ask you to complete a very detailed profile. This process can include completing onerous questionnaires about your dating preferences and habits, coming up with a detailed description of both yourself and your ideal match, and of course uploading flattering photos of yourself having fun in interesting locales. All this is to enable the "algorithm" to match you up with suitable candidates that it "thinks" are your perfect match. And it's all impacted by how well you know who you are looking for as your ideal match and what you are looking for in a relationship.

It's the same with your course. Who is your course for? Knowing who you are looking for is critical to your course-building journey. That should be a fairly easy question to answer. Right? And yet, despite the abundance of resources found by a simple Google search on "ideal customer," "customer avatar," and the like, course creators report that one of their greatest challenges is clearly identifying their ideal student avatar. In other words, the challenge is figuring out who the stand-in persona is that is held in mind when creating your course and marketing materials. Who's your ideal match?

The first mistake that course creators make is selecting a student avatar that is just way too broad. In an effort to keep the doors open to as many potential students as possible, they cast the net so wide that the avatar is something like "entrepreneurs," or "women," or "people who care about their health," or any other vaguely defined group. It's much too broad.

Another version of the broadly defined student avatar comes from the common fear that many course creators have of excluding perfectly good students who don't fit their ideal student description. This fear is what often leads you to nudge your way to a broader and less useful student avatar.

The Bullseye Analogy

Imagine you're holding a dart in your hand, taking aim at a board across the room. Your vision narrows to focus on the tiny red bullseye in the middle of the board. You lean slightly forward and make the most accurate shot you can muster. The dart hits the board with a thud, embedding itself two inches higher than the red bullseye, but squarely on the board. You didn't hit dead center, but it was still a good shot, worthy of celebration.

In this example, the red bullseye is your ideal student avatar. You won't always hit it and you can still celebrate the other students who find their way to you, but you still need to aim at the bullseye because you can't hit a fuzzy target.

But you shouldn't overcorrect, either, by going from not enough detail to having way too much detail by choosing a student avatar that is too narrow and specific. While you could download student avatar creation worksheets laden with questions about every facet of a hypothetical student and do your best to keep a real student in mind when you answer the questions, there's a lot you simply don't know about them. So you start making things up. Almost invariably, the result reads like that much-too-long online dating profile, so overloaded with information that it's hard to tell the relevant details from the red herrings.

What's the right amount of detail? The best ideal student avatars sit in the Goldilocks middle between too little detail and too much. They contain *just the right* amount of key details that allow you to bring a clear stereotype of your student to mind and nothing more.

An overly detailed and disjointed student avatar is like hearing someone's entire life story before meeting them. As the image in your mind of who they are becomes ever more detailed, it will correspond to who they actually are less and less. And as a result, your ability to predict what they will like and how they will behave will be impaired, rather than supported.

For a student avatar to be useful, you have to keep it firmly in the realm of caricature, where the mental picture of your target student is simple enough to give you a clear gut sense about what they like and how they will behave. So how do you do that? How do you go about choosing a target student?

The Casting Method

To help our students with this very challenge, Danny developed a technique that he calls the *Casting Method*. To get started, think of a character from popular media that could be a good representation of your ideal student. Not that they *are* your ideal student in every way, but that they have similar traits.

That will be the archetype for your ideal student—for example, Offred from *The Handmaid's Tale*, Claire Beauchamp from *Outlander*, or Dustin from *Stranger Things*. This method is so effective because a big part of the reason why so many people watch these shows is that they find the characters relatable—so you can trust that they're a good shortcut to describing a large enough swath of the population to support your business.

In other words, they're caricatures. Admittedly, no question about that. But they're caricatures of an archetype of a person that exists out there in the world. So if you pick a character in popular culture, you can trust there are enough people out there like that.

And there you have your shortcut to your ideal student. Remember what your ideal avatar is for: predicting what your students will like (and dislike), and how they will behave. It's not about having a seventy-page list of all their little quirks and knowing what they eat for breakfast. The purpose of having that avatar is so that you can quickly ask yourself helpful questions: Would my avatar like or dislike what I'm producing? Or would they be indifferent? How would they respond to this? If you match your ideal student to a popular character from pop culture, you'll quickly and pretty easily be able to answer that question.

As an example, let's look at Mirasee's ideal student avatar. In our case, it's Diane Lockhart, Christine Baranski's character on *The*

Good Wife and *The Good Fight*. If you're not familiar with the shows or the character, she is an attorney, although you can exchange that with any level of significant expertise. She's accomplished and intelligent. She's also starting something new and needing help. She's principled and driven to do work that is meaningful as well as rewarding. (Maybe just like you, dear reader?)

Now, we should share that when we explain the Casting Method, some of our students intuitively get it right away. They snap their fingers and say "oh, my ideal student is Joey from *Friends*" (or whatever), and they're off to the races. But many of our students take a bit longer—and if that's you, don't worry. Give yourself some time. This is an area where you can lean on AI to help you brainstorm—just prompt it with whatever you know about your ideal student and ask it for suggestions.

AI Prompts to Consider

I'm creating an online course about [topic], and I'm looking for a character from popular media to personify my ideal student. My student is [whatever you know about your ideal student]—what are some characters from popular television, movies, or books that could be good for me to use as my ideal student persona?

It's important to have a clear idea of your ideal student from the beginning. Think of it this way—if you only have a vague sense of who you want to attract, either you won't get any dates or that first date could end in disaster. And you don't want that. Knowing *who* you're after is a critical first step, but there's more work to do. Do you know what they truly *want*?

BUILDING SOMETHING THAT THEY WANT

When Heather was a young girl, she loved to create arts and crafts. Every year on her birthday her grandmother would give her a large box filled with all sorts of craft supplies that she had collected all year long specifically for Heather—things she knew that Heather would love to use to make something. And so it was called The Making Box.

The things you'd find in The Making Box weren't just the typical colored paper and glue and markers. It had special things like a colored feather, a unique button, a piece of velvet, a scrap of ribbon; things her grandmother had specifically chosen throughout the year to put in this special box. And Heather loved it; it was her favorite birthday gift every year. To other people, it may have looked like a box of junk, but to Heather, it was a box filled with ideas and magic. It was always the perfect gift no matter what the box held.

That's how you want your students to see your course: as the perfect gift designed just for them, as if you knew exactly what they wanted—because you did. But how do you know what your ideal student really wants and cares about in terms of both outcome and process? How do you know what they'd want as an overall experience of your course?

It isn't just about content. It's about the entire student journey, from the first moment they hear about you and your course to the completion and follow-up of the course and beyond. How you manage your student wants and needs along their learning journey matters.

If you have a sense of your ideal student avatar, you should already have a broad idea of what they want—and just as importantly, what they don't want. If your fitness program targets vegetarians, for example, you know they don't want meat-heavy menu plans that they have to figure out how to adjust. If your marketing course targets small-business owners, you know they probably don't want to know how to buy national television ads.

In other words, your student avatar can help you understand what your ideal student will find irrelevant, unhelpful, or beyond the scope of what they currently need. But in order to know what they actually do want, you need to do some more digging. You'll need to drill down several levels to uncover what your ideal student truly wants.

You could start by asking your potential students what they want. And in some ways, that's a great idea. But it will get you only so far; that's because there are two types of wants.

The first type is explicit—what people say they want. This is generally something you can gather by talking to people. Vegetarian fitness buffs might want appropriate menus and suggestions for eating enough protein and other nutrients. Small-business owners might want to know how to market locally in a way that doesn't break the bank.

But there's another type of want—implicit. These types of desires usually aren't expressed out loud or in so many words, and sometimes we're not even aware that they exist. For example, the people at Tesla realized that, explicitly, people wanted electric cars with a long battery life. That was pretty clear. But not many people were explicitly telling Tesla that they also wanted their car to parallel park itself or to come to them when called. And Tesla didn't stop at simply improving car features. They improved the entire car-buying experience (the customer journey) by taking out the dealer. Buyers can browse online, chat with someone if they wish, and order their car right from the comfort of their own home—never having to go to a dealer. If they want to test-drive a Tesla, the car comes to them.

AI Prompts to Consider

I'm creating an online course intended to serve [your ideal student]. What course topics might they be interested in? And what are the explicit and implicit desires that they might have in relation to those topics?

Many customers wouldn't have even realized this kind of thing was possible; other customers might not have said it out loud since it seems like a kind of unreasonable ask. Tesla tapped into people's implicit desires by loosening their imaginations. They asked people what they wanted, sure. But they also asked themselves what else was possible. Knowing your ideal student is more than simply having a list of demographics and what cereal they prefer. It's about creating your very own special box of course goodies (a course Making Box) just for them and truly knowing that it's exactly what they'd want.

MULTIPLE STAKEHOLDERS AND B2B

Back when Heather's two boys were teenagers, they all went on a family vacation. The thought was that since the boys were getting older, this was probably going to be the last chance for them all to have time to get away as a family. So they started planning a family vacation that included Heather's parents as well—six people each with very different wants and needs and different ideas on where they should go. They all agreed that it had to be somewhere hot (it was a winter vacation); there had to be a pool or beach; and there had to be a variety of things to do.

But that was where the agreement ended. Heather's parents had mobility issues, which meant restrictions on possible activities.

The two boys wanted more active things to do like snorkeling. The youngest was on the autism spectrum and needed a sense of consistency and routine each day. And Heather and her spouse mostly just wanted to relax by the water and see a different country. With all these different personalities, needs, and wants, the challenge was to figure out what would appeal to everyone enough that they all could enjoy the vacation. Maybe you've had a similar situation come up in your life.

The answer to this dilemma was a Caribbean cruise. Everyone slept in their same room every night so the consistency/home base box was checked. The itinerary went to multiple hot-weather countries over a span of a week, so the pool, beach, and warm weather box was checked. And it had a variety of activities for all ages and abilities—check and check. Everyone in the family got to choose an activity. They could go their separate ways at times but also have meals and some activities together each day. Everybody won.

It could be like that with your course. Some courses appeal to a single student and others involve multiple stakeholders. In other cases you are selling to a business rather than a consumer (the B2B market). So what do you do when you have multiple stakeholders? Do you choose a single customer avatar to go after (e.g., do you all go to Disney World because that's what the children want?) or do you try to appeal to them all (like Heather taking her family on a cruise to cover all their needs)? The answer depends on the relationship or lack thereof between stakeholders.

If they're independent of each other, then you have a choice of whether to appeal to one, some, or all of the stakeholders. You might choose to focus on a single avatar, such as your students. This is what we recommend to most businesses that have that option. Remember, every additional avatar has to be defined individually, which will likely add substantial complexity to the job of marketing and may create a dynamic of contradictory forces that lead to pleasing no one in pursuit of pleasing everyone. In other words, if you have a choice in the matter, it's best to start with a single student avatar and then add another one down the line if and when it makes sense to do so.

But your student avatars might not be independent of each other. Sometimes multiple student avatars make decisions as a unit, such as with parents and children or spouses (e.g., family vacation). In this case, we aren't talking about multiple students as much as we are about multiple stakeholders. You need all of the parties on board for the purchase to happen and each of the parties can essentially veto the deal. This dynamic is common when serving organizations where the end user and the payer may be different people and they also need a sign-off from someone else, or when creating offers for children since the child is the end user (student) and the parent is the customer.

AI Prompts to Consider

I'm creating an online course about [your topic] for [your ideal student]. Who are other stakeholders who might need to be bought in for them to sign up?

In these cases, you need all the stakeholders on board or you won't get any of them. You have no choice but to create avatars for each one and do the difficult work of creating a course that appeals to all of them. You'll need a course that they all want that has a benefit for all of them. In that case, it's even more important to be hyper-focused and targeted about who your ideal student is because the broader the definition of who they are, the harder it will be to create alignment with their needs.

If you're working in B2B markets, remember that business is made up of people. If you're able to build a real, meaningful relationship with the stakeholders, they're likely to see the value of your course. Understanding the wants and needs of multiple stakeholders can be tricky, but it's a necessary step toward success. Whether you choose to satisfy one stakeholder and go to Disney World or work to understand all your stakeholders and go on a Caribbean cruise is up to you, and it is also all part of the course-building process.

CHAPTER 8

Seed and Validate Demand

"Don't judge each day by the harvest you reap but by the seeds that you plant."

—*Robert Louis Stevenson*

IF YOU'VE EVER had a Lego fan in your life, you'll know that at some point they all dream of having that brilliant idea for a new Lego set that will make them millions—and it really can happen. Launched in 2008, Lego Ideas is a platform where Lego fans can submit ideas and vote for new Lego products that can then be turned into potential commercially available sets, with the original designer receiving 1% of the royalties. Fans compete for the coveted spots that could make them millionaires practically overnight. This process of co-creation with their users allows Lego to keep a close eye on what their audience wants, and delivers a steady stream of new product ideas.

While you don't need to go to the extremes that Lego does, you are going to use the same co-creation process to create your hybrid course. You've done the foundational work of committing to a solid vision and matching your ideal student to something they truly want; now it's time to make sure you are really on track with that idea.

And that's what you'll do next—research what your market really wants and seed the market. You'll speak to your ideal students to discover problem language (the ways they describe the problem you'd like to help them with). You'll do this primarily through personal conversations with people with whom you are already connected.

These conversations are critical for two reasons. One, they help you refine your ultimate course offer. This process of co-creation is an important part of the hybrid course process. And two, these conversations help you sow the seeds for a sales conversation later down the line with your prospective course participants (an added bonus is the possibility of attracting consulting or coaching clients down the road).

By the time your research is done, you'll have a good idea of the problem language people are using and whether or not your pilot idea will resonate with your market. You'll have made new connections and had fruitful and interesting conversations.

So what does this look like in practice? First you will put together a list of people you can contact for your market seeding and research conversations. You'll want to build out a list of thirty to fifty contacts you can reach out to so that you can end up with about fifteen to twenty research conversations.

The strength of your list will determine the acceptance rates for research conversations, the quality and depth of the conversations, and the number of warm leads you can go back to with an offer. So give building your outreach list the attention it needs.

In some cases, building out this initial list won't be too difficult—you can tap into your existing personal network. For example, let's say you're forty-five years old and your hybrid course idea is a program that helps adults speak with their aging parents about financial issues. If 10% of your three hundred Facebook friends are similar to you, that's thirty people right there, and adding relevant co-workers to get to forty or fifty should be pretty straightforward.

However, if your idea is a bit more targeted or you think you might not have enough contacts, you'll need to dig a bit deeper. Try looking more closely at your existing contacts (and who they are connected to) and asking for referrals. You could also expand your personal network by joining groups (online and in person) on your topic, or by contacting influential experts in your field.

If you already have an email list or an engaged social media following, these are the people you really want to talk to. Wherever possible, don't blast out an impersonal email asking about your new course idea. Instead, connect individually, with a personal touch. Reach out to people who have followed you from the very beginning, or who always leave comments on your posts, or superfans who buy all your products and give honest feedback.

AI Prompts to Consider

I'm creating an online course about [your topic] for [your ideal student]. Where can I reach people like that? Can you draft an email that I can use to approach them and invite them to a conversation to help me learn about their needs and interests? What are some questions that I could ask to help me understand what they might be looking for in a course?

Bottom line: what you're looking for are people you can actually reach out to for a conversation. With a little legwork, you should be able to grow your outreach list to at least thirty people fairly quickly.

Your next step is to conduct the actual conversations. Think of them as both research conversations and a part of your sales process. After all, they sow the seeds of your course in your potential student's mind. But you're not selling them anything right now! You're just asking questions and laying the groundwork.

So how do you go about conducting your conversations so that you're meeting the two objectives of research and building relationships? It helps to have a short list of questions ready. You want to understand your target audience's biggest challenge—what are the drivers of the problem, solutions they've tried, results they've gotten, and the ideal solution in a perfect world?

Then have a few follow-up questions ready for possible responses that respondents might give, especially for your first few calls. You can also just say "tell me more" if they say something that you find interesting and would like to learn more about.

While it's a good idea to try and cover as much as you can from your list of questions, you may not be able to cover all your questions on every call. That's okay. It's a good idea to identify a couple of important questions that you definitely want to ask, so that way even if you don't get to ask all your questions, you'll have covered the most important ones. You'll also find that each respondent is different, so you may learn a lot from some respondents, and others might not be as forthcoming or knowledgeable. That's okay too.

If you follow this process, you're learning from each conversation and developing a deep understanding of how your course idea resonates with people, how you might possibly revise it, and what language best captures how people think of their problem.

But how does it work if you serve the B2B market? Market seeding in B2B works just like the B2C (business-to-consumer) market. It's about building relationships and validating assumptions. However, if you're working in B2B markets, you'll need to have more research conversations, foster relationships with advocates within organizations, and be prepared to do extra networking. It can mean more work up front, but remember it takes a yes from only one or two organizations to fill your course down the road.

STRIKING WHILE THE IRON IS HOT

When a blacksmith works with iron, they heat it in order to make it malleable and then place it on an anvil and hammer it into shape. Of course, iron stays hot enough to work with for only a limited amount of time, so a blacksmith must strike while the iron is perfectly hot in order to be successful.

The same is true for your market seeding research. But we don't want you to think of it as market research, because that evokes the image of taking your time, and poring over spreadsheets of data.

A core part of what we're doing with seeding is creating context for your course. That context doesn't last forever, and today it lasts for less time than it used to. There's a ton of data out there showing that our ability to pay attention to things over time is declining. That means you have to do the seeding and research conversations quickly. If it takes months and months for you to do your seeding and market research, then by the time you circle back around, the context is gone and it's too late, and you lose a lot of the effect.

What's the time frame for conducting these conversations? Many people feel hesitant to send out that first email to set up a conversation. Others feel comfortable taking it slow and having these conversations gradually, spreading them out over many months. We get it—these are all very normal responses to stepping out of your comfort zone and doing something new. But, while we understand where these anxieties are coming from, it *is* important to take quick action and keep making progress.

Conducting your market seeding conversations needs to happen fast, ideally within two to four weeks. You need to keep your iron hot, so think of this as a sprint. Otherwise, it's possible to get stuck in this phase for months. The longer you stay stuck, the more likely you are to lose steam (and heat) and motivation about launching your course. Or if you do manage to stay motivated, you're putting a bigger window between the conversations and when you'll be ready to share your offer with students. This means that their need for your course may not be as urgent, or it just fades from their attention and your iron will be cold, making you too late.

Remember that there is a point of diminishing returns, beyond which additional conversations won't give you much incremental return for your time. This ensures that you're using the conversations to create a great offer and you're able to offer it to prospective students sooner rather than later. So strike while the iron is hot, set a timeline of about three weeks for these conversations, and treat this part of the process as a sprint.

IDENTIFY MINIMUM VIABLE SCOPE

The next step to finalizing your pilot idea is to make sure the focus and scope are as narrow as they can be. We do this by using a concept called the minimum viable outcome, which is basically about determining the smallest scope for your pilot that will still create an outcome your customers will be happy with. This is an important step, because for many of our students the instinct is to be as generous and helpful with their knowledge as they can be. So your initial vision for a pilot might be a lot longer and more complex than it needs to be.

But you have to remember the reason for piloting in the first place—you're validating a lot of assumptions, or hopes, including that people want to pay for what you're selling, that you can deliver the outcomes you're promising, and that you have enough passion for the topic to sustain you through the challenges of growing a business. It's a lot easier to validate these things when you keep the focus specific and narrow. Also, people taking your pilot generally don't want to become experts in your field. They just want the outcomes you're promising them. So teach them only what they absolutely need to know to get a result.

An easy way to zero in on an appropriate level of focus involves a thought exercise about a short plane ride from New York to Chicago. Imagine, if you will, that you arrive at the airport, go through security, and board your plane. You find your seat and fasten your seat belt. After the flight attendant has pointed out the door you just came in through and explained how to fasten the seat belt you've already fastened, the plane takes off and you're on your way. Just as the plane starts taxiing down the runway, you start chatting with the person sitting next to you. You immediately hit it off, and learn that they are your ideal student and in dire need of your help. You'd love to just give them access to your course, but you haven't created it yet. And you've got a busy schedule, so you just don't have time to help them one-on-one. This leaves you with the length of the flight, which is just over two hours long, to teach them as much as you can to provide that help and transform their lives. So what would you teach in those two hours that would create the biggest impact in their life?

This thought exercise is useful in arriving at a focus for your pilot course because it crystallizes your thinking around the minimum viable outcome that you can deliver that would still be meaningfully impactful to your students. You can then test your hypothesis in relatively short order, and maximize your chances of success by co-creating as much of the curriculum as possible with your actual students. Here are a few questions you can ask yourself to see if your focus is narrow enough:

1. **How long will my pilot have to be in order to deliver on this promise?** There are some exceptions, but in most cases pilots shouldn't be more than four to six weeks long. If you need much longer to deliver on your promise, you might want to scale back the scope.

2. **If someone were to start my pilot but quit after a month, would they see any benefits?** If so, what would those be? And how could you cram the most possible benefits into those first four weeks? Can you make those the only benefits offered in the pilot?

3. **If whatever you're doing for them is yielding results, what would be the first big milestone they would hit that would give them a real visceral sense that this is working?** If that milestone is so compelling, can you make it the entire promise of your pilot?

The point of these questions is to help you narrow down the scope and focus of what you'll offer. This makes it easier for you to deliver on your promise, and also creates a tighter and more focused promise that your audience is more likely to get excited about.

YOUR ONE-PAGE PILOT PLAN

Back in January 2006, Heather decided to run the Honolulu Marathon that was happening that December. Now, that may not seem like a mind-blowing decision, but Heather had never run a marathon before and, in fact, had never run one step in her life prior to that decision. How do you go about running a marathon never having run before? Well, you need a plan and a good one. So with the end goal of running and finishing the Honolulu Marathon in December 2006 in mind, Heather set out to create a plan that would ultimately get her to her goal.

Working back from the date of the marathon, she created a plan for herself that included learning how to run both short and long distances, building up her stamina, eating well, making a plan to get to Honolulu, and arranging childcare for her two children while she was gone, among other things. It was a detailed multistage plan. And it worked. On December 10, 2006, Heather crossed the finish line of the Honolulu Marathon, just one of over thirty-three thousand runners who would do so that year.

How did she do it? She began with the end in mind and knew exactly what she needed to do to get there. And that is what you need to do for your course. You have to decide what information you will actually present to your students; you need a plan.

The way people tend to start designing a course is to ask themselves, "What do I want to teach?" and "What do I want to include?" But it's not about what you want to teach. It's about what *they* (your students) want to learn.

You want to begin with the end in mind. Instructional designers call this backward integrated design: At the end of the course, what do you want your students to know? What do you want them to feel? What do you want them to experience? What do you want them to be able to do? You will need to go a few layers deep but first you must ask yourself what you want them to be able to do at the end of this whole process. What do they want to be able to do? It's about competence. It's also about how well you want them to be able to do it and under what circumstances, because those involve very different levels of training and preparation.

If you had asked Heather in January of 2006 if she could run, she might have been able to do a quick sprint to save her life. But running a full 42-km marathon and not passing out was out of the question. That's a very different level of skill and preparation, and the same applies to anything that you're teaching.

Consider the topic of active listening skills. Understanding what those skills are about is one thing. Being able to actually do it is another thing entirely—and being able to do it *well* is a whole other level beyond that. Do you want them to be able to perform an exercise in a controlled role-play situation? Or do you want them to use the skills in the middle of a heated argument, on a sensitive topic with someone that they're close to? All these situations require very different levels of skill, and therefore require very different levels of training.

With this in mind, think about what your students actually want to be able to do, how well they want to be able to do it, and under what circumstances. And remember that fundamentally, what people want is a shortcut: the more of a shortcut it is, the more valuable the course becomes.

Once you have the outcome that you know that they want, the next step is to work your way backward from that eventual goal to where they are now through a process called scaffolding. The idea of scaffolding is that new knowledge is always built on top of existing knowledge, information, and ideas. People don't learn something new and understand in a vacuum; they understand it as it relates to things that they already know, and this applies to all kinds of things.

You don't want to take for granted any underlying concept assumptions and ideas that people may or may not know. It's about vocabulary and fluency with words and phrases, but also with ideas and concepts.

So how do you figure that out? Well, you can do it by creating a mind map. Start with the outcome that you want to deliver in the middle of the map and then pull out of that the things your students need to know in order to create this outcome. Then for each of those things, you go out another ring, asking yourself each time, "What do they need to know in order to be able to understand that?" Keep working outward until you've reached a level where you can assume and trust that they will just know that piece of information.

AI Prompts to Consider

I'm teaching a course about [your topic] to [your ideal student]. The end goal that they want is to be able to [your outcome]. What are the prerequisite knowledge and skills that they will need in order to be able to learn these skills?

It doesn't matter how interesting or how fascinating you find something; if it's not on the mind map, it doesn't need to be in the curriculum. Mind maps can be great for exploring how concepts relate, but they don't work very well for outlining a curriculum, because a curriculum is linear, meaning that people go through it one lesson at a time. So you need to take that mind map and convert it into a list. You do this in three steps.

1. **First list out the broad topics in order.** This rough outline is your one-page plan. Essentially the course is about the big outcome and then each lesson is about one of the big steps to that outcome encapsulated with a specific deliverable. So you work backward from the end.

2. **Next, flesh out what you need to cover for each lesson.** Use bullet points (sub-item one, sub-item two, etc.) for each lesson.

3. **For each lesson, you've got the big objective** of what your students will achieve, and the sub-items are the building blocks (those things that you want to make sure you include and cover in your course).

This list is all you need as a working outline for your course, i.e. your one-page pilot plan. Of course there's more detail that will need to be worked out, but that comes after you've already enrolled your first cohort of paying students.

CHAPTER 9
Enroll Paying Students

"Selling is helping people do what they're already inclined to do."

—*Daniel H. Pink*

HEATHER FIRST BECAME a coach long before coaching was a "thing" in Canada. In fact, she'd never even heard of it until someone asked her to be their coach and help them transform various parts of their life. But it was the perfect entrepreneurial path for Heather, as she had been doing it unknowingly (and unpaid) for years. The big challenge came when the job she was in didn't like that she had a side gig, so she took a big risk and quit that job. But, as a single mom, she had two young children to look after, a house and mortgage, car payment, and all the other usual bills that needed paying. She needed paying clients and fast.

So what did she do? Well, she hustled, and in less than sixty days she had twenty new coaching clients, and you could say that at that point her coaching business was officially launched. But in order to find and enroll those new clients, she had to sell her services. She had to get on the phone and speak to real people about her offer. It was a constant roller coaster of emotions: fear, elation, disappointment, gratitude, more fear, doubt, frustration, and, ultimately, joy. With zero real sales experience, she fumbled through it with some great successes and some utter failures too, but she learned and pivoted through the entire process, and that made all the difference.

And you can do the same. You've worked so hard to get to this point. Now it's time to proudly present your offer to your market, confident that you're addressing and delivering the transformation they most desire. You won't be pushy or try to sell when it's not a good fit. You've done great research, and you know you have something that can really help people. The right people will be delighted to enroll in your course.

It's true that selling can be exciting, but it can also be intimidating, frustrating, and nerve-racking. Selling is important for many reasons. First of all, it's important from a business standpoint—if you don't sell your course, you won't make any money, your business will not be sustainable, you'll be out of business fairly quickly, and you won't be able to pay your bills.

Selling is also very important from a program design perspective. When you sell your course and work with students, you gain clarity and validation that your course is something that people really want and are willing to pay for. If you give your course away or do not charge a premium price, you won't gain that clarity, and you'll never know if your course is truly viable from a business perspective. That's why it's so important to sell your course and why it's especially important to sell it *before* you build. You don't want to put in all the time and expense to build something that no one wants. What is selling, really? Let's find out.

CONCENTRIC CIRCLE OF CONNECTION

Have you ever had a Girl Guide (or Girl Scout, if you're American) cookie? If you're like most of us, you've had more than one of these decadent delights and probably have a favorite or two. As a young Girl Guide, Heather used to both look forward to and dread the cookie sales time of year. She looked forward to it because . . . it's cookies, and what's not to like, right? But she also dreaded the sales part. Going door-to-door asking family, friends, and strangers if they wanted a box of cookies was a lot of work and rather nerve-racking, and, frankly, not everyone was kind.

But despite all that, she almost always won the award for most cookies sold in her unit because 1) her competitive nature made her persevere (she was highly self-motivated and committed to win); 2) she had a wide range of family and friends ready to buy; and 3) she wasn't afraid to ask for a sale from anyone who would talk to her. She carried those cookies with her everywhere she went and would offer a box to pretty much everyone she met. As the years went on, her confidence grew and the sales lessons she had learned as a child set her up for the life of an entrepreneur.

What do cookies have to do with selling your course? More than you might think, especially when it comes to where you go to sell your course. You see, it doesn't matter if you are selling cookies or courses, the same principle applies for how you find customers and where you go to offer your product.

Think of it as three circles. The inner circle is made up of your friends and family—those people who know you best and who trust you. Then, outside that circle, you have referrals—the people that those who already know and trust you have referred to you (think friends of friends). Finally, the outer circle is strangers; ideally, you save them for last.

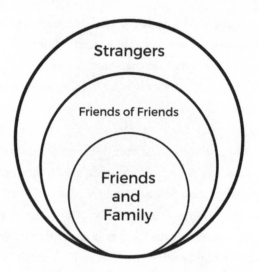

When it comes to enrolling students for your course, you want to start at the inner circle and work your way outward because at this stage in your course-building process, you are still figuring things out and validating your assumptions. You want to start with those who already know and trust you (sometimes called "low-hanging fruit") and who may be a little more forgiving. Also, it's not fair to exclude the people closest to you from your best offers. It takes more work to warm up a stranger. Since you are trying to launch this quickly, start with those closest to you and referrals.

SELLING AS AN ACT OF SERVICE

Have you ever gone to a car dealership and bought a new car? If you have, chances are that you've had either a really great experienceor a really terrible experience. The pushy car salesperson stereotype exists for a reason. Unfortunately, while many car companies are trying to change this impression, that is still the norm rather than the exception. That is *not* the kind of selling you will be doing for your course.

Let's get clear on the rules of ethical selling: You only sell if you think it's best for the other person and they only buy from you if they think it's best for them. The selling process should be a shared exploration that is meant to create shared clarity. Tactically speaking, it's about helping your potential student to see their present (where they're at now) and future (their ultimate goal), the gap between the two, the obstacles they need to overcome to get to their future, and how your course fits and bridges that gap.

Before getting to a place where they're ready to invest a substantial amount of time, money, and energy in anything, there are things that your future student needs to know, understand, and believe about the broader opportunity of the course, about themselves, and of course about you and your offer. All these things must be communicated to your ideal prospect before they will be ready to become your ideal student.

There are a *lot* of ways that you can sell. It can be as technically complex as bots and automated messages or as involved as a webinar or multiday event or anything in between. And those are all good strategies that have their place. But when you're getting started, especially for your first few runs, you always want your bias to be toward simplicity . . . keeping it simple!

To enroll students, there are two groups of people you'll want to reach out to: people you talked to when you did your market seeding and demand validation, and those you didn't.

Ideally, when making an offer to someone, you'll want to have introduced the idea of your course topic to them first because it predisposes them to be receptive to hearing the offer. Generally speaking, this means you've already earned their attention and interest. Remember the idea of co-creation that we talked about earlier? Selling is another area where the genius of co-creation comes into play. This is the perfect time to go back to those people you initially spoke to and give them the opportunity to co-create the course with you. That said, you can also introduce your offer the first time you talk to someone and do it in a way that's not aggressive or pushy.

There are two broad approaches to selling that you'll want to explore. The first is a phone or Zoom call, and the second is an email conversation. Everybody wants to sell by email without having to talk to people. But trust us when we say that if it's feasible, a call is the better bet. You could also simply have an in-person conversation.

But before you can have a conversation, you need to reach out to request it—and unless you have a very close relationship with someone, it's no longer appropriate to just call someone out of the blue. It's more respectful to reach out with an email, text, or social media message and request to chat. Ultimately, you'll want to have a verbal conversation with them because you want to be able to explain what you're doing and then hear their unfiltered response.

One critical thing to remember here is that you want to contact people individually! You can use a template that you personalize for each contact, but never send a mass email; you're trying to build relationships, so keep it personal. All you're asking for is 10–15 minutes of their time to tell them about the new project you're working on, get their feedback, and see if they'd be interested—and if they aren't, that's totally fine, so it's a very low-pressure "ask" to make.

AI Prompts to Consider

Create an email template that I can use as a customizable base, inviting them to a conversation where I can tell them about my new course about [your topic]. I want the email to be short, and make it really easy for them to say "yes"—and we can coordinate logistics as a second step.

The email should be short and make it easy for someone to say "yes"—and then you can coordinate the logistics as a second step. If you ask them to coordinate logistics in the first email, responding takes more effort for them, and they're more likely to put the email aside and forget about it. This way, they'll reply saying yes, and then they're a little more committed when it comes time to coordinate the call, which you can do manually or use a scheduling tool.

Regardless of how you do it, the basic conversation is framed as a request for feedback and input on your course offer. It's that simple! To recap:

- Reach out to people on an individual basis, asking if they'd be interested in a quick call regarding your course topic.
- They'll respond and either say yes or no.
- If they say no, thank them for their time; if it's yes, say "great" and propose a meeting time or send them a link to your scheduling tool.

Reaching out for a sales call is another place where it's easy to get bogged down. You might find yourself obsessing over the wording of your email, second-guessing your contact list, or finding ways to delay hitting that "send" button. Our advice here is just to do it.

Start by drafting a version of the email you plan to send to your prospects. Then add in some personal touches and send the email to *one* prospect on your list. Get that first one out of the way, and the rest will flow more easily.

Once you've set up your sales conversations, then it's just a matter of doing them. On these calls (whether you use the phone or a platform like Zoom), you'll first want to introduce the idea. If they are interested in learning more, then you explain the details, and then you ask them if they want to join. Be clear and specific! Don't use a generic question ("Are you interested?") and don't shyly add the request at the end of a rambling sentence. It's important to always tie it back to how the elements of your course will help them get results. The more they can picture the results, the easier it will be for them to commit.

Whether it's in person, on the phone, on Zoom, or via email, the process of having a sales conversation is straightforward. Working up the courage to actually make the calls is another story. Most people get very anxious about making these calls. Take some time to prepare yourself and practice.

Keep in mind that selling is an act of service. You are serving your students when you enroll them. When a person steps up and invests in themselves, gets out of their comfort zone, takes responsibility for their life, and *asks* for help, you serve them by leading them through the process. Every conversation you have with a potential student is all about serving the other person, whether they join your course or not.

When you understand that you earn more and have a bigger impact when you come from a place of service, you can feel good about everything you do. You won't dread the sales calls. You'll know you are helping people and enriching their lives whether they decide to move forward with you or not.

SELLING TO ORGANIZATIONS (B2C VS. B2B)

Of the thousands upon thousands of students we've had the privilege of supporting, about a third operate in B2B environments—meaning that they sell their services and programs to organizations rather than individuals. And while it's true that fundamentally every buyer is a person, there are differences in process and experience when you're selling to an organization with a complex approval process, multiple stakeholders, and budgetary constraints.

But that's not to say that it can't be done or even that it's particularly difficult. But it is different; what may work in one context may not work in another, which means that if you try to apply the same processes as you would in the B2C world, it may not work very well. Ultimately, it all boils down to the balance of power: Who can make the final decision to buy?

We'll get to the key differences between selling in B2B and B2C markets shortly. But first, let's go over the similarities:

- You're still selling to people, so focus on the relationships you've been building, and have personal conversations.
- You're still running a course and your main goal is to validate that people want and can achieve the transformation you're offering.
- You're still following the same basic sales process: decide on a price per student; create a clear and compelling offer outline; schedule and conduct sales conversations; and evaluate your results.

Your B2B sales process isn't radically different, but there are some additional factors to consider. Let's look at three: a longer sales cycle; customization; and crafting an offer outline for multiple stakeholders.

First, in B2B markets, you'll likely have a longer sales cycle. Even if the people you've had conversations with seem on board, they might not be authorized to say yes right away. Your course offering might have to work its way up multiple levels, or your contacts might have to wait several weeks before they can bring it up at a meeting. Because organizational decisions can take time, you should not put a deadline on your offer, otherwise you're likely to just get a no.

You can still establish urgency with your offer, however, without tying it to a deadline. You'll be able to create this urgency because you've done thorough high-touch research and can speak to the severity of the problem and how its effects are felt through money, productivity, or morale. How you frame your offer is what creates the urgency, rather than an arbitrary deadline.

Second, be prepared to customize your offer. This is a great selling point if you're competing with large training organizations: You can offer a personal touch that large-scale trainings cannot. You've spoken with people in the organization and have heard firsthand the unique dimensions of the problem. As such, you're able to address their specific needs much more robustly than an impersonal video course available to thousands of other organizations.

Finally, craft your offer and course outline to address the concerns of multiple stakeholders. As you analyzed your market research, you pulled out the problem language these stakeholders used. Now, turn that language into a clear and compelling offer. What were the concerns of the financial decision-makers? You might include a section called "Investments" in your offer outline that addresses the costs and associated benefits of your course. What were the concerns of the human resources–type people? They might care more about how your course will enhance employee development or morale, or improve retention. You might include a section called "Situation Analysis," where you reiterate the problems employees are facing and emphasize how your program can help solve those problems. In addition, think about your potential students within the organization. While they might not have decision-making power, they can advocate to the people who do make the decisions. This part of your offer outline will be similar to selling to B2C students— focus on the transformation you can help them achieve and show what concrete changes they can expect either in themselves or in their work environment. You could call this section "Goals" or even "Transformations."

Creating a complex offer outline that addresses the concerns of multiple stakeholders can feel like a lot of extra work. Selling in B2B markets takes longer and involves extra steps, but it can have really big payoffs. So keep at it.

CHAPTER 10

Hybrid Course Delivery

"Kids, in life there are a lot of big romantic moments and they make life worth living. But here is the problem: moments pass. And lurking just around the corner from those moments is a cruel unshaven bastard named Reality."
—*Future Ted,* How I Met Your Mother

THERE'S A CULINARY SCHOOL in the town where Heather lives. It's a school for aspiring chefs, sommeliers, and those wishing to enter the hospitality industry. Once a year, they put on an extravagant eight-course dinner to showcase their talents. The chef students plan and prepare eight delectable dishes—each about three bites. The sommelier students pair delicious wines with each dish. And the hospitality students serve each course. It's a choreographed dance where each student has a role to play.

If you attend this dinner, you can expect to experience fabulous food and wine. But there's also a little lesson built in, when the chef students come out and describe the choices they made for the food and the sommelier students educate you about their wine pairings. The servers are friendly, attentive, and efficient—exactly what you'd want from a night out. The experience itself is better than many highly rated restaurants. But here's the thing: It's their first time doing it. It's their pilot.

You can imagine that back in the kitchen chaos is probably reigning with people scrambling, dishes being dropped, and food being spilled. It's messy. But you'd never know it from your seat in the dining hall. As the customer, you only see the perfection of the experience because you don't know what's going wrong (if anything) behind the scenes. You can safely bet that students are learning valuable lessons that night and that next time they put on a dinner, they will make it even better.

You will experience a similar process with your course. As with all things, your idealized picture will be a bit different from the messy reality—but it's on you to make that messy reality great.

SHOW UP AND OVER-DELIVER

This is it—your moment of truth, the moment of transformation, where you actually work with people to get the result you promised. Just as with the culinary students, it's now your turn to show up, over-deliver, and shine. You've done your research, crafted an offer that resonates with your audience, and sold spots in your pilot course. You've used instructional design principles to craft a clear outline of your content. It's time to deliver your pilot course!

Recall back when we covered outlining your curriculum in three stages—the lesson outline, then the sub-item outline, then the actual draft—that we mentioned it would be improved upon later? Well, now is the time.

High-touch pilots can be a lot of work—but it's fun and rewarding work—so go into it with a positive attitude and embrace the journey. Yes, you are overinvesting at this stage. However, the insight you'll gain about how to create successful outcomes for your students is invaluable, and the joy of seeing students transform and overcome real problems makes all the work worthwhile. It's time to show up and embrace the work as you deliver (and over-deliver) your pilot course. There are three reasons for this:

1. **It's short-term.** While working more hours and pushing yourself much harder than you're used to isn't sustainable over a year, remember that this is a hard four to six weeks, and then you're done.

2. **It leads to course success.** Putting the extra effort into your pilot now will save time and money down the line if you choose to turn your idea into a full course.

3. **It leads to student success.** One of the most important things to do in your pilot is to pay close attention to where your students seem to "get it" and where they have questions. Being aware of and responding to their needs makes it more likely that they'll see the outcomes they desire.

Over-delivering on value sets you up for the transformation and profit flywheel—it leads to happy students, which leads to results, which leads to glowing testimonials and case studies, which can lead to more students, more results, and so on. So yes, now is the time to hustle, show up, and over-deliver, and doing that requires that you stay nimble.

STAYING NIMBLE

Have you ever watched a professional ballroom dancing performance? If you haven't, we highly recommend it. Watching the dancers can be breathtaking. They are light on their feet and agile—extremely nimble and they seemingly float on the air as they flawlessly move around the room and effortlessly adjust to the changes in the music. But sometimes, one of the dancers misses a step or the music isn't just right, and when those challenges present themselves, the dancers have two choices: they can either keep dancing or give up and leave the dance floor. Which choice will you make?

No matter how prepared you are, challenges will inevitably arise as you deliver your pilot course. Remember, you've made some assumptions along this journey and some will be wrong. As you deal with challenges, evaluate your own communication and actions to make them clearer in the future *and* draw firm but empathetic boundaries for what your students can realistically expect from your pilot. Stay nimble, ready to adapt on the fly, and see every challenge as a learning opportunity.

Let's look at some common challenges that could occur. Misaligned expectations come up when somewhere along the way, someone got the idea that you could do something for them that you can't, or didn't plan to. If one student has expectations that don't align with what you've promised, the issue is probably with the student. But if several people misunderstand in the same way, then odds are it's a communication problem on your end.

Whatever the cause, there are a couple of ways you can handle this. First, you may need to adapt your lessons by adding or changing some material. We recommend doing this especially if it was your mistake that caused the problem. Remember that ultimately, your goal is to help your students succeed, so if you need to change some things around, go ahead and do it.

Second, if it's not possible to change the scope—or if you feel like you don't need to—then set clear expectations and boundaries.

Address the misunderstanding, explain what you actually promised, and say what you can and cannot do moving forward. In short, if you've miscommunicated, do what you can to fix it. You may need to "overcommunicate" at this point, which is fine. If students have unrealistic expectations, draw boundaries firmly but empathetically.

Another potential occurrence is seeing spikes and drop-offs in participation. Imagine you've been running your pilot for a couple of weeks and you're getting into the swing of things. But then one morning you wake up, and you have several emails in your inbox—all of them from students who are having a new and sudden difficulty. Sit up and take notice, because something important is going on!

If there's a sudden spike like this in student activity, one of two things has happened: 1) you shared something really interesting and people are thrilled and excited, or 2) something went wrong—either they're not understanding something, or there's a problem with the technology.

If you see a sudden drop-off, that's significant too. Maybe people got frustrated with not understanding things, you missed the mark on what a good next step for them would be, or they just aren't seeing results. No matter the cause, assess the situation: What happened immediately before the spike or the drop-off? What lesson did they just go through? What was their homework? Did they get access to all the files and resources they needed?

Figuring it out might be as easy as identifying a typo in an email you sent them, or a particularly challenging bit of homework. If you can't figure out what caused the sudden shift in behavior, ask your students. Tell them the truth—that there was a big upswing or drop-off in the level of interaction, and you'd like to know why and what you can do to help them. Whatever the problem turns out to be, fixing it should be a top priority so you and your students can continue moving toward the objectives of the pilot.

You may need to change your initial plans when this happens because if your pilot group doesn't understand what you're teaching them, you can't move on to the next topic until they've mastered it. This is where it's important to be responsive and flexible.

Another problem that could arise doesn't sound so bad: an over-abundance of enthusiasm. However, if you consistently get a lot more interaction, excitement, and engagement than you were planning for, it can take more time and energy than you had originally budgeted. This is a pretty good problem to have. It means that your students are really engaged and excited to be on this journey with you, and you're going to get lots of great information about what they do and don't understand, what they care about, and what they're annoyed by.

And here's a bonus—the questions and concerns your current students have are likely to be questions and concerns your future students will have, so you'll be ahead of the game next time. Note where you should elaborate on a concept the next time around; write down questions that a lot of students have and begin compiling a Frequently Asked Questions document. Take in all the enthusiasm, gather the energy to address all the comments and questions in the short term, and look forward to turning it into great content in the longer term.

Being able to adapt on the fly and stay nimble as challenges arise as you deliver your pilot course will pay big dividends down the road. Adapting to help your pilot students as things come up will also help your future students and your future course.

AFTER THE PILOT: PIVOT, ITERATE, OR SCALE

It's been a long and winding road, and you've finally made it to the other side! You've chosen the topic of your pilot, narrowed it down to a minimum viable outcome, and created your one-page plan. You reached out to likely prospects and enrolled some of them in your pilot. And then the real work began, with the delivery of your ideas. The process was exciting and exhilarating, with both ups and downs. But now it's done. The pilot has been delivered, and it's time to take stock and decide what you should do next. There are three dimensions on which you'll want to evaluate the pilot:

1. **Student outcomes.** Before they signed up for the pilot, you made promises about the outcomes that your students could look forward to. How has that played out? Are your students happy and satisfied? Are you proud to tell others about their outcomes?

2. **Financial performance.** Did you make as much money as you had hoped with the pilot? Was it financially successful beyond your wildest dreams? Did it just meet your expectations? Or was it a disappointment?

3. **Your experience.** At the end of the day, it's very important for you to enjoy your work. So did you enjoy the experience of delivering your pilot? Was it more fun than you ever expected? Was it stressful and frustrating?

Now, in evaluating your pilot, remember that your first attempt at anything is bound to be messy—that's exactly why we pilot rather than buildout a full course from scratch. It stands to reason, then, that the results of your pilot on these three dimensions are likely to be mixed: not terrible, but not always amazing, either. And that's perfectly fine, because you don't want to evaluate the pilot based on how it went, but rather by how it would go the next time, informed by what you've learned.

In other words, knowing what you now do, how would it go if you did it again? Do you feel confident that the next time you deliver this training it will be a smashing success on all fronts? Do you have ideas about how to make it great that still need to be validated? Or was the experience such that the biggest takeaway was to never, ever try that again? That is unlikely, but much better for you to learn that sooner rather than later!

The relatively rare worst-case scenario is that you will have learned that this is not the path for you to take, so your next step should be to pivot to a new idea. Go back to the drawing board, find a new topic and direction, and start over. And while you're at it, celebrate that it took you only a few months to learn this, rather than the years that it takes so many entrepreneurs!

Sometimes, you'll find that you have an idea of how to make it great, but you need to validate it to be sure. In that case, your next step is to deliver a second pilot course. Change everything that you think needs to be changed, validate your assumptions, and go from there. And often, you will have learned enough from the pilot that you are now confident in your abilities to deliver an excellent course to a larger number of students.

CHAPTER 11

Scale: Reaching for More

*"I'm a dreamer. I have to dream and reach for the stars, and if
I miss a star then I grab a handful of clouds."*

—*Mike Tyson*

KEVIN PLANK started the company Under Armour with his personal savings and five different credit cards. Within a year of starting the company, he was broke and deep in credit card debt. His big break came when he sold his clothing to Georgia Tech for $17,000. His product began to take off and was used by NFL teams and picked up by major retailers. And so he scaled the business over time, and today, Under Armour is a billion-dollar brand.

At long last, you're ready—you have a concept that you've validated that people want and are eager to pay for, that delivers great outcomes, and that you enjoy—now it's time to make it bigger. In other words, it's time to go from online course to online course empire.

This is where your dreams really can come true. Recall the intention and vision that you created at the beginning of this journey? You committed to creating more leverage, freedom, and impact than you currently have. This is where that truly starts to happen, and it is a function of scaling three things: fulfillment, marketing, and the business.

SCALING FULFILLMENT (PROCESSES AND PEOPLE)

When Mirasee was a much younger and smaller company, course fulfillment was done mostly by Danny himself. But as we grew (and in order to grow), it wasn't optimal or practical for Danny to do all the course delivery on his own. And so a small team was created to support the student learning journey and overall fulfillment. Over the years, not only has that team grown, but Danny also now calls on other leaders in the company to support with content creation, coaching, and delivery. We're constantly scaling our fulfillment processes and systems so that we can serve more students.

Ultimately, the question now is how do you fulfill your course so that you can support more and more students? Scaling fulfillment is where you really get to start tweaking the sliders of the different dimensions of hybrid. Do you add team members or other types of student support? Do you change how you present the course materials (evergreen vs. live)? Do you automate certain parts of the student experience?

The process of scaling fulfillment starts by looking at everything that you did during your pilot to create a great experience for your students. Then you want to optimize the best parts of that.

First, optimize the overall student experience and smooth out any rough edges. This is when you spend the time and money for things like working out any content kinks, creating professional videos, properly formatting your resources, and perfecting onboarding procedures. Look at your overall student learning journey from start to finish and make it as smooth and professional as possible for your students.

Second, improve your course content and student experience based on the feedback you received during your pilot—this is the heart of co-creation. Review the feedback you received and decide if the feedback is realistic and viable. You don't have to implement every piece of feedback. Remember that you are the expert and the owner of the course. Make the changes that make the most sense and that will positively impact the most students.

Finally, don't think about doing *less*, but rather about doing *more* but in a way that is scalable. When you scale delivery, you are offering your students more value, a fuller experience. That doesn't mean you are working harder; it means that the course and the systems you have in place are working harder. This is your fully polished, mature course—the one with all the bells and whistles—the course you are charging a premium price for. Take a look and decide where you can offer more value.

It's important to scale your delivery capabilities because ultimately you want to be supporting a much larger volume of students. But for that to happen, you also need to scale your marketing.

SCALING MARKETING (CULTIVATING AN AUDIENCE)

A recent lead conversion study found some interesting stats about people who make contact with a company for information and what happens when they do. The study found that just over half of the people who inquire about something eventually buy what they inquire about within the next eighteen months. However, the study found that only 15% of them buy in the first ninety days, leaving 85% of the buyers in the "more than 90-day" category. The thing about an online course business is that it's only as good as the number of students that you can reach. If you're trying to be profitable on just that up-front moment from your pilot course, you're working with a hand tied behind your back.

Scaling marketing all comes back to business math, specifically, what it costs to acquire a customer. The goal of scaling marketing is to reduce that customer acquisition cost by optimizing what already worked when enrolling your pilot students. So that means fine-tuning your messaging, maybe having it reworked by a professional copywriter, improving the design, leaning into stronger conversions, and dropping the parts of the process that didn't work. This is something that you want to start working on once your pilot is validated and you know who you're serving.

You might be able to get away with not doing this if you have unfair advantages such as celebrity status, early mover, or prime placement, but even then you're leaving a lot of money and transformation on the table.

To scale marketing, you have to address two key things: first, how do you attract a steady flow of leads and students; and second, how do you engage the students you have?

Adjusting your lead attraction (also known as lead generation) lever means consistently going where your potential students are and presenting them with something attractive, something they want that solves a problem they are facing, and then turning them into students (customers).

And the thing about optimizing your efficacy at turning leads into students means that you can suddenly afford to invest in more and more expensive marketing channels. The better you're doing with your sales, the more money you have, and therefore you can go into more expensive marketing channels. You get even more reach and exposure, and so on and so forth. The more you can afford to spend, the more that is suddenly within your reach, whether it's running paid ads, creating a podcast, doing content for SEO, or any number of other things.

And that makes a huge difference. But there's another lever when it comes to scaling your marketing, and that is engagement. You do this by growing an audience and nurturing it through channels such as content and email marketing.

When you have an audience, it means that you don't have to start from scratch to attract new people each time you want to make a sale because when you do a promotion, there will be people who don't buy, but will hang around to learn more from you, and eventually buy later, just as we saw with the lead conversion study. So building that audience engagement really changes the game for you.

Scaling delivery and scaling marketing are great, and they create a really strong economic engine for your business. But there's another dimension of scale for us to look at, which is scaling the business as a whole.

SCALING THE BUSINESS (CUSTOMER LEARNING JOURNEY)

The story of Apple is legendary: two guys with high school diplomas, lots of motivation, and hours of sweat equity coming together to change the world. Shaggy, hipster Steve Jobs and his code geek friend Steve Wozniak worked together in Jobs's parents' garage in the early 1970s, building personal computers in their spare time. In 1976, the two of them completed their first product—the Apple I computer.

You'd never guess that within five years, they'd have one of the hottest tech companies around. It started with just one offering, the personal computer. Then over time, other products were added to the mix such as the iMac, iPod, iPad, and iPhone. Today, iMac and iPhone users are some of the most loyal tech users in the industry. New data from analysts at Consumer Intelligence Research Partners shows that Apple fans continue to remain loyal to Apple, with 90% of iPhone buyers remaining with Apple. Now that's brand loyalty.

When it comes to scaling your business, you may not be an Apple—but remember, it's much easier to sell again to raving fans (i.e., existing students) than it is to find new ones. Once students complete your pilot, you'll want to be able to work with them again. So developing long-term relationships with your students to increase their Customer Lifetime Value—the amount of revenue you get from one student over time—is critical to scaling your business. You'll do this by building out a path of increasingly valuable offers and building out the support structures for your full hybrid course.

Right now, you've produced or are working on producing a hybrid course. That's critical work in scaling your business. But, as you've seen, getting people's attention can be really tricky! The process of attracting and converting new students can be time-consuming, expensive, and frustrating. You have to lay a lot of groundwork to take people on a mental and emotional journey, so that they trust you as an authority and believe that your offer will truly work for them.

But as you scale your course and run it a few times, you're also creating a new customer base—your existing students already know you, trust your expertise, and have experienced firsthand that your offer really works. So you want to have more to offer them. And that's why it's so important to design a retention path with a series of offers that will keep your students coming back for more, and experiencing deeper and deeper transformations.

So let's talk about designing your retention path. The first point is that this is an actual path, not simply a collection of offers. Each offer should ascend, both in terms of price and the transformation it promises. Just like you want to reduce the friction students experience going through your course, you also want to reduce their friction moving along your retention path. Your offers should have a natural flow, one to the next, so that they make sense to your students. Each offer should address the next set of problems, questions, or desires that result from their new level or awareness and skill.

Let's take a quick look at the retention path of Ruzuku, one of Mirasee's portfolio companies. We start with a free gift: *5 Steps to Your Online Course*. This establishes trust and provides quick wins for our audience. Then we have the *30 Days to Your Online Course* program for people just starting out. Most people in this program have an idea for a course but don't know how to get started. For people who are ready to move forward after this, we have *No Empty Seats*, which helps people launch and market their courses. From there, a few people will want a more personalized experience to dive deeper into marketing, and for that, they can book a private consultation with Abe Crystal, the company CEO.

So if you want your path to really make sense to your students, you need to take some time to understand what they really want. And the best way to do this is to pay careful attention to their feedback. You already have the feedback you collected from your pilot. Were there places you could expand into a new offer, or more complex questions that kept coming up? Where did your students get stuck or want more information? Those are the places that make for another great step along your retention path. After you've pinpointed your students' other frustration points and desires, you can start to build out the offers that will make up your retention path.

A great example of this is creating a membership or community. This brings people together around a focused theme or common interest, and they can be free or paid. You might start a free Facebook group that focuses on a certain issue. You could include valuable content, inspiring posts, and opportunities for discussion. With a paid membership, you'll up the value. You could include online workshops, guest experts, and more of your own participation in the discussion, for example. With the free or relatively low-cost nature of most membership groups, you can expect lower engagement and higher turnover, so you'll want a plan in place to keep inviting people in to replenish and grow the membership.

The nature of being an entrepreneur means that sooner or later, you're going to have another idea for how you might create something that makes the world a little bit better (or a lot better!) for the people that you serve. And when that happens, it's time to gear up to do this whole process all over again.

And that means working your way again through everything that we covered, from committing to your new vision, matching a new target student to the transformation you offer, building something they want, seeding the market with demand, creating a narrative of co-creation, designing your pilot hybrid course, and enrolling paying students, to scaling delivery, marketing, and the business.

So what's possible? How big and how fast you grow is up to you. Go back to your initial vision for yourself and your business. Imagine yourself with everything you dreamed of—positively impacting more and more students, sharing your message, making a difference in their lives—but also imagine your lifestyle, working less but making more. A hybrid course empire is possible. But it's up to you to make it happen.

Focus on Transformation

"Act as if what you do makes a difference. It does."
—William James

THE WORLD OF ONLINE COURSES AND AI is fluid and constantly evolving, and we're just at the very beginning—with many exciting possibilities on the horizon. And it's easy to be dazzled by what might come next. Will we have AI tutors, perfect in their knowledge, and versatile in their teaching? Maybe one day. Will we have virtual classrooms where learning is as easy as dreaming? Only time will tell.

But remember the fundamental truth, that your best bet is to focus on the things that will never change. Whatever new and novel technologies might emerge, and whatever opportunities they might create, people will always want transformation, and you will always stand to win by offering a shortcut that gets them there in less time, at less cost, and with less risk of failure.

And of course, we will continue to pay attention, and update our communities—so be sure to grab the resources we've created for you (link on the next page) and watch for our updates. The path of progress may be unpredictable, but we will do our best to stay informed and keep you up to date.

But ultimately, and no matter how sophisticated the technology becomes, the learning will still happen in the brain that is behind the eyes of the person using it. And in the end, the impact of any new technology will depend on how well it can cater to these enduring needs.

So focus on transformation. Be the guide on the side, who is there to support students in achieving the outcomes that they care about. Remember that for every course created, every lesson planned, every piece of feedback given, every improvement made, if it's in service of the student, you're heading in the right direction. At the heart of this journey into the unknown, it is not just about following the path of progress but also about ensuring that progress is meaningful—because in the grand design of things, what we do matters.

Claim Your Free "Online Courses and AI" Success Bundle

We've created a special bonus resources package to support you in applying the ideas in this book to build and launch your own online course business:

✓ **Hybrid Courses Bootcamp video training series**

✓ **Audiobook of Danny's bestseller *Effortless***

✓ **Library of our most commonly used AI prompts for course building**

This entire resource bundle is our no-cost-whatsoever gift to you.

→GO TO MRSE.CO/GUIDE-RESOURCES TO CLAIM IT!

It's a Team Sport

WRITING A BOOK IS A TEAM SPORT. Of course, there are the four of us who wrote the book—but without many great people around us, we wouldn't have the knowledge or experience about which to write, the time or focus to put proverbial pen to paper, or even the logistical support to turn our typo-riddled manuscript into the near-pristine work that you hold in your hand. So yes, there are a lot of people to thank!

Topping the list are the wonderful people that we get to work with every day at Mirasee, where we teach coaches, consultants, and expert entrepreneurs to teach their gift and grow their businesses—and of course the students that we have the privilege of working with, supporting, and also learning from.

Deep gratitude also to Ally Machate and the entire publishing team behind her at The Writer's Ally. Thank you for making the book in our hands better than we imagined it would be in our minds.

And most of all, our families—for their understanding, support, and reminders that despite how much we might hate parts of the writing process, there would be a light at the end of the tunnel. So to Bhoomi, Priya, and Micah, to May and Hanna, to Larry, Ryan, and Devon, and to Angela, Riah, and Lillian—thank you!

About the Authors

DANNY INY is the founder and CEO of the online business education company Mirasee, whose work on strategy training won special recognition from *Fast Company* as a "World Changing Idea." He has been featured in the *Harvard Business Review* and *Entrepreneur*, and contributes regularly to publications including *Inc.*, *Forbes*, and *Business Insider*. He has spoken at institutions like Yale University and organizations like Google, and is the author of multiple books about online courses and business, including two editions of *Teach and Grow Rich* (in 2015 and 2017), *Leveraged Learning* (in 2018), *Teach Your Gift* (in 2020), and *Effortless* and *Online Courses* (in 2021). He lives in Montreal, Canada, with his wife, Bhoomi (who is his partner in both life and business), and their children Priya and Micah.

HEATHER E. WILSON helps coaches worldwide build and scale their businesses so they can do their magic and change the world. As Director of Education at Mirasee, Heather develops course curriculum, and trains and supports the coaching team to ensure an amazing student experience. She also loves celebrating student wins, cheering them on as their confidence—and success!—grow.

A business coaching expert and speaker with more than twenty years of experience in instructional design and online course innovation, Heather is the author of *Your Life According to You*. She was also a business coaching pioneer when the Canadian industry first began. And she founded and ran a highly popular Canadian coaching community for many years, which has evolved into the present-day Confident Coach Community.

Warrior, change-maker, risk-taker, and adventurer all rolled into one, Heather lives on the east coast province of Prince Edward Island, Canada. She's the mother of two boys, loves traveling and listening to Bon Jovi, adores a great gin cocktail . . . and will try just about anything once.

ARI INY started working for Mirasee in the summer of 2014 when they needed a new Facebook ad coordinator, and joined the team full-time six months later in order to expand the company's Facebook presence. Since then, Ari's role within Mirasee has evolved a number of times—he's become the head of HR for the company, Mastermind facilitator (where he learned how to do business coaching firsthand from Danny), Partner Liaison, and ACES Coach.

Before joining Mirasee, Ari jumped around quite a bit. After being released from the army, he worked in a bookstore chain where he was eventually promoted to managing a store, and then two stores (fortunately, they were close to one another!). After that he joined a Facebook game start-up, where he picked up a bunch of valuable skills, including Facebook marketing.

When not supporting the Mirasee team and his students, Ari enjoys spending time with his beautiful wife, playing with their dog, reading epic fantasy (and lots of other kinds of fiction too!), playing video games, and sleeping. ;-)

ELIZABETH LEE taught undergraduate philosophy for eight years before realizing that she liked everything about teaching . . . except for the teaching itself. So she swapped her university post for a more behind-the-scenes role at Mirasee, where she enjoys designing courses, organizing ideas, and letting someone else do the teaching!

Elizabeth enjoys traveling, swimming, playing with her two children, and eating sour candy.